THE QUESTIONABLE CASE FOR EASING SUDAN SANCTIONS

HEARING

BEFORE THE

SUBCOMMITTEE ON AFRICA, GLOBAL HEALTH, GLOBAL HUMAN RIGHTS, AND INTERNATIONAL ORGANIZATIONS

OF THE

COMMITTEE ON FOREIGN AFFAIRS HOUSE OF REPRESENTATIVES

ONE HUNDRED FIFTEENTH CONGRESS

FIRST SESSION

APRIL 26, 2017

Serial No. 115–21

Printed for the use of the Committee on Foreign Affairs

Available via the World Wide Web: http://www.foreignaffairs.house.gov/ or http://www.gpo.gov/fdsys/

U.S. GOVERNMENT PUBLISHING OFFICE

25–260PDF   WASHINGTON : 2017

For sale by the Superintendent of Documents, U.S. Government Publishing Office
Internet: bookstore.gpo.gov   Phone: toll free (866) 512–1800; DC area (202) 512–1800
Fax: (202) 512–2104   Mail: Stop IDCC, Washington, DC 20402–0001

COMMITTEE ON FOREIGN AFFAIRS

EDWARD R. ROYCE, California, *Chairman*

CHRISTOPHER H. SMITH, New Jersey
ILEANA ROS-LEHTINEN, Florida
DANA ROHRABACHER, California
STEVE CHABOT, Ohio
JOE WILSON, South Carolina
MICHAEL T. McCAUL, Texas
TED POE, Texas
DARRELL E. ISSA, California
TOM MARINO, Pennsylvania
JEFF DUNCAN, South Carolina
MO BROOKS, Alabama
PAUL COOK, California
SCOTT PERRY, Pennsylvania
RON DeSANTIS, Florida
MARK MEADOWS, North Carolina
TED S. YOHO, Florida
ADAM KINZINGER, Illinois
LEE M. ZELDIN, New York
DANIEL M. DONOVAN, JR., New York
F. JAMES SENSENBRENNER, JR.,
  Wisconsin
ANN WAGNER, Missouri
BRIAN J. MAST, Florida
FRANCIS ROONEY, Florida
BRIAN K. FITZPATRICK, Pennsylvania
THOMAS A. GARRETT, JR., Virginia

ELIOT L. ENGEL, New York
BRAD SHERMAN, California
GREGORY W. MEEKS, New York
ALBIO SIRES, New Jersey
GERALD E. CONNOLLY, Virginia
THEODORE E. DEUTCH, Florida
KAREN BASS, California
WILLIAM R. KEATING, Massachusetts
DAVID N. CICILLINE, Rhode Island
AMI BERA, California
LOIS FRANKEL, Florida
TULSI GABBARD, Hawaii
JOAQUIN CASTRO, Texas
ROBIN L. KELLY, Illinois
BRENDAN F. BOYLE, Pennsylvania
DINA TITUS, Nevada
NORMA J. TORRES, California
BRADLEY SCOTT SCHNEIDER, Illinois
THOMAS R. SUOZZI, New York
ADRIANO ESPAILLAT, New York
TED LIEU, California

AMY PORTER, *Chief of Staff*   THOMAS SHEEHY, *Staff Director*

JASON STEINBAUM, *Democratic Staff Director*

———————

SUBCOMMITTEE ON AFRICA, GLOBAL HEALTH, GLOBAL HUMAN RIGHTS, AND
INTERNATIONAL ORGANIZATIONS

CHRISTOPHER H. SMITH, New Jersey, *Chairman*

MARK MEADOWS, North Carolina
DANIEL M. DONOVAN, JR., New York
F. JAMES SENSENBRENNER, JR.,
  Wisconsin
THOMAS A. GARRETT, JR., Virginia

KAREN BASS, California
AMI BERA, California
JOAQUIN CASTRO, Texas
THOMAS R. SUOZZI, New York

(II)

CONTENTS

THE QUESTIONABLE CASE FOR EASING SUDAN SANCTIONS

WEDNESDAY, APRIL 26, 2017

HOUSE OF REPRESENTATIVES,
SUBCOMMITTEE ON AFRICA, GLOBAL HEALTH,
GLOBAL HUMAN RIGHTS, AND INTERNATIONAL ORGANIZATIONS,
COMMITTEE ON FOREIGN AFFAIRS,
Washington, DC.

The subcommittee met, pursuant to notice, at 2:30 p.m., in room 2200 Rayburn House Office Building, Hon. Christopher H. Smith (chairman of the subcommittee) presiding.

Mr. SMITH. The subcommittee will come to order.

Good afternoon, everybody, and welcome and thank you for being here. We will be joined shortly by Ranking Member Bass and other members of the subcommittee but we do have votes scheduled for 3:15. There will be a brief break for that. Then we will come back and conclude the testimonies from our distinguished witnesses.

For most of the 37 years that I've been in Congress, the House and Senate have been heavily involved in U.S. policy toward Sudan. For example, I've chaired 12 congressional hearings including two markups on Sudan since 1996.

My first hearing focused on child slavery in Sudan and we actually had witnesses who had been slaves there and many others—NGOs who spoke of this egregious practice—followed by genocide hearings in the Darfur region, the persistent bombing of people in the Nuba Mountains, the Khartoum government's failure to abide by the 2011 agreement that created an independent South Sudan, and, of course, myriad human rights violations and the government's historic relationship with terrorist groups.

The Sudanese Government has long sought sanctions relief in Congress and successive administrations have considered such relief as an incentive for Khartoum to reach and abide by various peace agreements.

When I, joined by Greg Simpkins, our staff director, personally met with President Bashir in Khartoum in August 2005, I spoke about Darfur refugees and visited two of the refugee camps, Mukjar and Kalma camp, and spoke almost exclusively during the 1½ hour plus meeting about ending the violence. President Bashir, on the other hand, focused almost exclusively on sanctions relief.

The Obama administration, in its last days in office in January, purported to see justification in ending a sanctions regime built over decades. In its announcement on the easing of sanctions, the Obama administration declared positive actions by the Sudanese

Government in five key areas. One, rebuilding counterterrorism cooperation; two, countering the threat of the Lord's Resistance Army; three, ending negative involvement in South Sudan's conflict—one of our witnesses will testify later negative involvement was never really defined; four, sustaining a unilateral cessation of hostilities in Darfur, South Kordofan, and the Blue Nile provinces; and five, improving humanitarian access throughout Sudan.

Missing in this list of positive developments are improvements in the overall human rights situation in Sudan including and especially sex and labor trafficking, and I would remind our friends who are here at this hearing and my colleagues, Sudan is a Tier 3 country on the State Department's list. So it is an egregious violator and the narrative in the report is an indictment, frankly, of both sex and labor trafficking.

On religious freedom, Sudan continues to get a failing grade as well from the State Department and has been designated, again, a country of particular concern, or CPC, which subjects it to other sanctions.

It is well within the government's ability to meet the standards in the five areas mentioned and I would hope other areas as well if it truly has the will to do so.

However, the Government of Sudan has never been known for its respect of the rights of those not considered Arab, such as Darfur residents, who were persecuted despite being largely Muslim, or Sudanese who were not Muslim at all.

There was the case in 2014 of Meriam Ibrahim, a Christian woman sentenced to death by a Sudanese court for refusing to renounce her Christian faith. The court also ordered Ibrahim, who married a Christian man in 2011 and was 8 months pregnant when she was arrested and imprisoned, to receive 100 lashes for adultery because her marriage was considered void under Sharia law.

The couple had a child, a 20-month-old boy, who was also in detention with her. Imagine that, a 20-month-old boy in detention next to her, behind bars.

I joined with a group of House and Senate members including one of our subcommittee's members, Congressman Meadows, in working with elements of the Sudanese Government in the eventually successful effort to vacate the sentence and allow Ms. Ibrahim and her family to come to the United States.

That effort demonstrated and perhaps highlighted that there are some elements of an internally divided Sudanese Government with whom we can work with toward a better future for Sudan's people.

But it also confirms that other elements are viciously opposed to religious freedom and other fundamental human rights.

The Obama administration's justification of its decision on sanctions relief was done in the absence of any congressional consultation and presented as a fait accompli.

It freed more than $30 million in unfrozen Sudanese assets, allows commercial transactions in all sectors and singled a new policy of more positively reviewing licenses to do business in Sudan. Commercial transactions prohibited as a result of the Government of Sudan's designation as a State Sponsor of Terrorism and Darfur-specific targeted actions are still in place.

The entire sanctions easing process will be fully effective 6 months from the date of announcement, 6 months from January 13th.

Today's hearing is intended to begin asking the hard questions concerning sanctions relief in order to facilitate improved relations between the U.S. and Sudan if that will benefit the people of Sudan.

Nevertheless, it's incumbent upon the U.S. Government to honestly consider the conditions under which sanctions easing is justified.

As stated earlier, the Government of Sudan is fully capable of meeting the requirements outlined in the January Executive order but we must be sure of the extent to which that government is abiding by them and urge them to do more when necessary.

Various reports indicate that attacks on civilians including, sexual-based violence, continues by government and allied forces.

Even though human rights improvement is not one of the requirements in the Executive order by the former President, we must not as a government ignore this aspect.

Successful administrations and Congresses have worked hard to ensure that human rights concerns in Sudan are addressed.

And I would note parenthetically in this room back in the year 2000 I presided as chairman of this committee over the markup of the Sudan Peace Act.

This has been a totally comprehensive and bipartisan effort over the years and, again, human rights is essential if we are to truly help the people of Sudan. Now is not the time to abandon decades of work, as I said, by men and women of good will in our Government and many American citizens who have supported our efforts.

We must also not forsake the welfare of the people of Sudan for whom our efforts all this time have been made.

If the Government of Sudan is indeed willing to work with us to fulfill the aspects mentioned in the executive order and improve the state of human rights in Sudan, then for the sake of the Sudanese people our Government should make the effort to work with them.

But it will do the Government of Sudan and its people no good if we turn a blind eye to ongoing problems and fail to press for genuine improvements that are sustainable and that can be clearly demonstrated.

As we await the appointment of the Trump administration officials tasked with making the ultimate decisions on these matters, the clock is ticking.

We have assembled a panel of private sector witnesses who can give us an expert look, a picture, of the status and the adherence to the requirements outlined in the Executive order and human rights in Sudan. We do not have a witness that is involved in humanitarian activities—we asked a few—because of their concern, and it's a justified concern, had they spoken out and done so with the candor that they would do that that could limit their ability to do business and to provide humanitarian relief inside of Sudan.

This hearing is only the beginning of Congress' investigation into the matter. By July 12th, when the sanctions easing regime fully comes to fruition or into effect, we hope to know whether there is sufficient justification to approve this action or whether more work needs to be done.

So this is a timely hearing, I believe. Again, we have a panel of truly remarkable witnesses who are extremely knowledgeable and for that I am very grateful for you being here today.

And I'd like to yield to my friend and colleague, the ranking member, Ms. Bass.

Okay. I'll yield to Mr. Garrett.

Mr. GARRETT. Very briefly, Mr. Chairman, I just wanted to take this opportunity to articulate my concurrence with your assessment of the situation but also to note the progress that's been made on a case that somewhat parallels that of Meriam Ibrahim and that being the case of Czech pastor Petr Jasek as well as two Sudanese counterparts, Hassan Abduraheem and Abdulmonem Abdumawla, who are currently held in the Republic of Sudan.

I will say that my experience working directly with Maowia Khalid, the Ambassador of the Republic of Sudan to the United States, has been extremely fruitful and that the Sudanese representation here in Washington has been very forthcoming and cooperative as it relates to our concerns in this instance and we look forward to a positive outcome in those cases.

That notwithstanding, obviously, there are any number of steps to be taken, moving forward. But I do believe and I want to articulate that establishing good faith and positive working relationships will actually help facilitate progress as Sudan works to move itself back into the mainstream of nations.

And with that, I would yield back my time and thank you.

Mr. SMITH. I would like to yield to Mr. Suozzi.

Mr. SUOZZI. Mr. Chairman, I am just waiting to listen to the witnesses. Thank you.

Mr. SMITH. Mr. Donovan.

Mr. DONOVAN. Thank you, Chairman. I just wanted to thank you for conducting this important hearing. With votes coming sometime within the next 20 minutes I'll yield my time for the witnesses.

Mr. SMITH. Thank you very much, Mr. Donovan.

I would like to welcome our witnesses to the witness table, beginning first our witness up will be Ambassador Princeton Lyman. He's a senior advisor to the President of the United States Institute of Peace.

He served as U.S. Special Envoy for Sudan and South Sudan from 2011 to 2013. As Special Envoy, he led U.S. policy in helping in the implementation of the 2005 Comprehensive Peace Agreement. His career in government has included assignments as Deputy Assistant Secretary of State for African Affairs, U.S. Ambassador to Nigeria and South Africa and Assistant Secretary of State for International Organizations.

He began his government career with USAID and served as its director in Ethiopia. He has testified several times before this subcommittee. We always are so glad to welcome him back and to welcome his insights and his wisdom.

We will then hear from Mr. Brad Brooks-Rubin, who serves as the policy director for The Sentry and as policy advisor to the Enough Project. In this capacity, he helps to lead the efforts of The Sentry to disrupt the corrupt networks that fund and profit from genocide or other mass atrocities in Africa. From 2009 to 2013, Mr. Brooks-Rubin served as the Special Advisor for Conflict Diamonds in the United States Department of State.

While there, he also contributed to the U.S. efforts related to conflict minerals in eastern Congo, particularly in the area of corporate due diligence.

Prior to joining the Department, he served as an Attorney-Advisor in the Treasury Department's Office of the Chief Counsel on Foreign Assets Control.

Then we will hear from Mr. David Dettoni, who is the director of operations for the Sudan Relief Fund and the managing director of TSA, a German-based organization, created to assist the lives of the people of Africa, particularly the people of Sudan and South Sudan.

Previously, he was director of operations and outreach at the U.S. Commission on International Religious Freedom and a senior legislative assistant to Representative Frank Wolf. He assisted Chairman Wolf in foreign policy, national security, and global human rights initiatives and was co-staff director of the Congressional Human Rights Caucus.

And then we will hear from Mr. Mohamed Abubakr, of the African Middle Eastern Leadership Project. He's a human rights activist with more than a decade of experience in the nonprofit sector. He has founded and served as director for multiple NGOs focused on humanitarian relief, human rights, youth empowerment, and peace programs across the Middle East and Africa. He has been hosted by many universities to address students on a variety of topics.

In 2016, he launched the African Middle Eastern Leadership Project, or AMEL, the Arabic word for hope, a U.S.-based nonprofit organization that seeks to empower young leaders from the Middle East and Africa to build pluralistic societies.

Ambassador Lyman, please proceed.

STATEMENT OF THE HONORABLE PRINCETON N. LYMAN, SENIOR ADVISOR TO THE PRESIDENT, UNITED STATES INSTITUTE OF PEACE

Ambassador LYMAN. There we go. Thank you very much, Mr. Chairman, Ranking Member Karen Bass, other members of the subcommittee.

This subcommittee has, over the years, been extraordinarily attentive to the issues of Sudan and South Sudan. For those of us who work on it, we are very grateful and I know you've had a major impact on the thinking and the policies in this area.

Mr. Chairman, nothing is easy when it comes to policy for Sudan. It's not a nice government. It's a government that has committed major violations of human rights. It restricts free speech and assembly. It has resisted democratic reforms. It has carried out actions against its own people in many parts of the country. Indeed, since its independence it has been ruled in a system by various governments where power and wealth is at the center and the outlying areas are marginalized either through warfare, co-optation or both.

And at the same time, Sudan is a major country in this area—not just in the Horn, but in northern Africa, in the Sahel and in spite of the sanctions over many years and over attempts by rebels to overthrow it, this government is not collapsing. The future of Sudan is very much in its hands.

So how do we reconcile these things? How do we reconcile and deal with this almost dilemma? The fundamental problem, in my view, Mr. Chairman, is that this government has to at some point find its way to the path of reform without thinking that that's a zero sum game—that it's not afraid to undertake the kind of reforms that would bring peace, prosperity, and democracy to the country.

Other autocratic regimes have done this. South Korea did it. South Africa did it. Spain did it. Indonesia did it.

Right now, there are some people in the Government of Sudan who recognize there are a lot of people who don't or don't want to or think the task is too great—the risks are too great.

So what do we do? Where is our role in this? We have leverage. We have leverage because of sanctions.

As you pointed out, Mr. Chairman, it's a big issue for the Government of Sudan. But sanctions are only leverage if they are not static—if they are used—if they are part of a process.

Now, I realize that, as you pointed out and I know our witnesses—very, very knowledgeable people—will indicate the imperfections not only in this situation but the limitation of the tracks that you mentioned.

We are talking about—I won't comment on the intelligence one—I don't have the information on that—the Lord's Resistance Army—unfortunately, both Uganda and the United States are pulling back on that.

But the two that are most controversial are the limited amounts of progress on humanitarian access and the peace process—the cease fires.

But I look at this differently. I look at this as a very limited opening of a dialogue. We haven't had a dialogue on these issues since 2013.

They closed it off after the end of the South Sudan independence, and we have and the administration have to work hard to open it. It's limited on both ends. It isn't the big road map all the way to perfect relations. We have tried that in the past. Too difficult, too complicated, too many variables.

It starts limited five tracks that have a lot of limitations. But the sanctions are also limited that are being lifted.

Yes, they open up some trade and they do a number of things. But they are not going to lead to a lot of investment in South Sudan. There are too many variables. It doesn't include debt relief. It doesn't include State Sponsor of Terrorism. It doesn't include all the legislative sanctions which are in place. So it's limited on both ends and the Sudanese, they know that, too.

So the question is where do we go with this dialogue? Obviously, you want them to at least perform on the five tracks that are put out there.

But the big question, which you've raised, Mr. Chairman, and others have talked about, is how do you get to the other issues—

the human rights issues, the real peace process issues—and that, to me, is what we should be working on for past July, whether they, hopefully, make these and what comes next and what degree of sanctions additional otherwise one might move? It has to include human rights and freedom of assembly. It has to open that door to dialogue and further work on the peace process.

I would just make two other points. We forget the role of the opposition. They are players here and they control the agenda as well.

The Darfur opposition is in disarray. Its leaders are all in Paris. The SPLM-North is having a split. They have put restrictions on humanitarian access that I do not find logical.

They are part of the process. They have to agree to cooperate as well and I think we have to give attention to them and what their positions are—listen very carefully, because they have a right to be suspicious, but at the same time question where we think they are wrong.

I would make one other recommendation, Mr. Chairman. We have a lot of restrictions on our USAID program in Sudan. It can work in humanitarian areas. Its development areas are only along the border in very limited areas.

Supposing you gave USAID a little more freedom, a little more flexibility, so that these sanctions which allow more medicine, more agricultural inputs to come in, they could partner with NGOs in Sudan and other groups.

Make sure that those goods are getting out to clinics in the outer area, getting out to farmers outside—they don't get concentrated at the center. So we are opening up the economic system at the same time we are opening up a little of the political system.

So I see this as a first step, an opening. It's part of a dialogue. It's going to be a long way to go. It's more like Burma than others, and I think in that sense I think it's the right move even though it's fraught with all of the problems you raise.

Thank you.

[The prepared statement of Ambassador Lyman follows:]

United States Institute of Peace

The Questionable Case for Easing Sudan Sanctions

Testimony before the House Foreign Affairs Subcommittee on Africa, Global Health, Global Human Rights, and International Organizations

Ambassador (rtd) Princeton N. Lyman
Senior Advisor
United States Institute of Peace

April 26, 2017

Chairman Smith, Ranking Member Bass, and members of the Subcommittee, thank you for holding this hearing on Sudan. This Subcommittee has consistently followed and helped shape U.S. policy on Sudan and South Sudan over many years. I am pleased to have been asked to testify today. The views I express are my own and not those of the U.S. Institute of Peace, where I am a Senior Advisor.

Nothing is easy when it comes to U.S. policy toward Sudan. On the one hand, we are dealing with a government which has committed major human rights violations, restricts free speech and assembly, and has resisted the kind of democratic reform that would bring peace and prosperity to the country as a whole. Sudan remains, indeed has been since its independence in 1956, a country in which power and wealth are concentrated among groups at the center with the outlying regions kept at bay by being marginalized, coopted, or fought against, or sometimes all three.

And yet, at the same time, Sudan is a major country in the region, not just of the Horn, but in northern Africa and the Sahel. It is a major player in the crisis in South Sudan. And as much as the U.S. has sanctioned the government and its leaders, and as much as rebels have fought to overthrow this government, the current government is not collapsing and the future of Sudan is very much in its hands. I would argue that simple collapse or forceful overthrow of the government would not achieve U.S. fundamental objectives; almost surely not produce the peace, democracy, or prosperity that the people deserve.

So how do we reconcile these factors, i.e., that the government is objectionable in so many of its ways, and that it is nevertheless an important player in a region of great importance to us?

The fundamental problem in Sudan is that those in power, especially those focused most of all on the security of the regime, are wedded to the traditional form of governance I described earlier. The risks of change to them appear too great. The challenge is for the government to realize that there are pathways to peace, inclusiveness, democracy, and respect for human rights, that are not a zero-sum game, i.e. not one in which the current government's constituents lose and others alone gain. Other autocratic governments have found those paths and have undergone transformations successfully. South Korea, Spain, Indonesia, South Africa are just some examples. Only by undertaking those paths of change can Sudan escape from its current condition of endless internal wars and limited development.

What is the way the U.S. can have the most effective impact to help bring about change in Sudan?

One of the advantages is that the government of Sudan is deeply concerned with its relationship with the U.S. This is primarily the result of the U.S sanctions that constrict its economy, isolate it politically, and limit its options. But sanctions are only useful if they help bring about change. After decades of sanctions, they have not ended government autocracy, settled the war in Darfur, resolved the conflict in the Two Areas, or security cooperation. Some would argue that more sanctions will bring this government to basic transformation. But while sanctions can help move governments to policy changes, even major ones like Sudan giving independence to South Sudan, autocratic governments do not commit political suicide because of sanctions.

Furthermore, sanctions give us leverage, but not if they are static. U.S. policy should be focused on ways to bring about commitment in the government and its supporters as well as the opposition to undertake the transformation needed. This requires serious in-depth dialogue. Sanctions give us leverage in such a dialogue, but only if sanctions are on the table.

That brings us to the focus of this hearing: the Obama administration's initiative to lift some Sudan sanctions against some important but still quite limited benchmarks.

The U.S. has not had a constructive dialogue with the Government of Sudan since 2013 when it engaged in the final stages of resolving the issues between Sudan and South Sudan. The Government of Sudan was largely impervious to one. This latest initiative, based on patient, hard work by the U.S., has reopened the dialogue. It is wisely not based on a full roadmap to normalized relations. Past experience shows us that too many intervening events and still wide differences undermine that kind of roadmap with Sudan. Instead, we have a limited set of benchmarks and a still limited lifting of sanctions. It is an opening, not more, not less.

The benchmarks are indeed limited. I will not comment on the intelligence track. The regional commitment against the Lord's Resistance Army seems to be fading on its own, unfortunately, with both the U.S. and Uganda pulling back. On South Sudan, the Government has restricted support to the opposition, but the peace process in South Sudan is much more complex than that. The U.S. will need a more intensive international effort to make progress there.

The most controversial benchmarks are those for humanitarian access and a cease-fire. The benchmark for humanitarian access is surely but a small beginning to true access. We will need to see from the humanitarian organizations if the changes being taken produce results. The cease-fire is holding overall but not without violations in a volatile atmosphere. That brings me to an important factor that critics of this initiative tend to avoid. Both greater progress on humanitarian access and progress toward a real peace process in both Darfur and the Two Areas depend not only on the government but also on the armed opposition. Right now, the armed opposition is divided and in Darfur it is in disarray.

About Darfur, the Justice and Equality Movement (JEM) engaged itself in the civil war in South Sudan and was badly mauled. The Sudanese Liberation Army (SLA)/Minnie Minnawi is now engaged more in Libya than in Darfur. A sign of their general weakness on the ground is that all three Darfurian opposition leaders once again reside in Paris. The Sudan Revolutionary Front (SRF) – an alliance of the Sudan People's Liberation Movement (SPLM)-N and the Darfurian opposition has largely fallen apart. There are splits now within the SPLM-N which itself has been unable to resist becoming involved in the South Sudan civil war.

In this atmosphere, the SPLM-N has been as obstructive of an agreement on humanitarian access to the Two Areas as the Government of Sudan. One of its conditions is that some of the aid must come from outside Sudan, i.e. through Ethiopia. It is hard to see this as more important than getting badly needed humanitarian aid to a population that has been fighting for six years without regular access to the outside world. I suspect that this issue is more a mirage, that the leadership of the SPLM-N is not comfortable yet in participating in the kind of dialogues and political process being offered in the roadmap for change being propounded by the Africa Union High Level Panel on Implementation (AUHIP), headed by Thabo Mbeki. This is where much work needs to be done with the SPLM-N as well as with the Government of Sudan.

None of this is to excuse the Government of Sudan. Its military assaults account for much of the weaknesses of the Darfurian opposition groups. And it could easily agree to some aid coming from Ethiopia to break that deadlock. But the point is that using sanctions against the Government of Sudan to resolve these complex conflicts will not be sufficient without regard to the role of the opposition.

As for the sanctions, which have been suspended and which could be ended in July, they are less than it seems. Yes, they will open up trade and spark interest in investments. But with all the other sanctions in place, and continuing Sudan's status on the list of states sponsoring terrorism, it is doubtful that much long-term investment will take place. Financial institutions will remain wary, and investors will need more long term assurances. Debt relief is not on the table either.

In sum, this is an opening to a serious dialogue, a means to promoting serious political reform in Sudan. It is a small but important opening. Leveraging sanctions has helped open that door, with relatively little cost. The key question to be asked is where it might lead. That takes us to what happens after July, especially if the five benchmarks are met.

Next Steps

One of the principal criticisms of this initiative is that is leaves out any requirements by the Government of Sudan for free speech and assembly, a free press, release of political prisoners, and other steps that would allow for true political debate and broad-based participation. These must be part of the next phase of dialogue and any further lifting of sanctions. These are the issues that pose the greatest test for the Sudanese leadership about whether it is prepared to embark on significant transformation of the political system. There is no consensus within the Sudanese leadership on this matter. So, there will need to be intense debate, discussion, and resolve to move forward. The U.S. can be an important part of this process. Sanctions give the U.S. entrée and leverage. But they have to be used strategically not bluntly. Work on this next phase should be going on now, within the U.S. government and with the Government of Sudan.

Second, there must be serious dialogue with the armed opposition. Its disarray, internal disputes, and hard lines are not serving the situation well. The U.S. can play an important role here too, balancing its dialogue with the Government of Sudan with its work with the opposition. Advocacy groups who are in regular contact with these groups should not be shy to confront them about their weaknesses and perhaps misdirected policies.

Finally, there is something Congress can do to help make the trade openings taking place beneficial to the people of Sudan, not just to the elite. Currently USAID is under restrictions on development work outside conflict and border areas. USAID should be given authority to work more broadly in the fields of agriculture, health, and education to steer the opening of imports in these sectors to those most in need. Through its own programs, public-private partnerships, support of Sudanese NGOs, and other means, USAID could get nutrition, health and education out beyond the center. This is another way to leverage our sanctions, when lifting them, to take complementary steps to open the economic as well as political system.

In conclusion, the initiative under way with Sudan is an opening to a more serious and intensive dialogue with the Government of Sudan about peace, democracy, and development. It is not the U.S job alone, for it is central to the mandate of the AUHIP, and most important essential to the people of Sudan. But sanctions give the U.S. leverage. The U.S. needs to use them strategically. And we need to recognize that U.S. objectives, the conditions for lifting them, relate to fundamental political and security factors that have long operated in Sudan. The U.S. needs to embark on an engagement in Sudan that is conscious of the dimensions of change it is seeking and the challenges they present to the parties in Sudan. It will of necessity be a step by step process. But engagement is the only way to move the process forward. This recent initiative is one small but important step in that direction.

The views expressed in this testimony are those of the author and not the U.S. Institute of Peace.

Mr. SMITH. Thank you so very much, and without objection all of your full statements and anything you want to attach to it will be made a part of the record.

Mr. Brooks-Rubin.

STATEMENT OF MR. BRAD BROOKS-RUBIN, POLICY DIRECTOR, THE SENTRY

Mr. BROOKS-RUBIN. Thank you. Chairman Smith, Ranking Member Bass, members of the subcommittee, thank you for holding this important hearing and providing the Enough Project and our financial investigative initiative, The Sentry, with the opportunity to share our perspective on a country that has long vexed U.S. policymakers.

As the chairman noted, Congress has a deep and bipartisan history of leading U.S. efforts to promote peace, human rights, religious freedom, and counterterrorism objectives in Sudan, and this is an absolutely critical moment for Congress to continue that engagement.

It is a critical moment because this past January, as has been noted, in the waning moments of the last administration an all-or-nothing choice on economic sanctions on Sudan was created—either maintain the 2-decades-old comprehensive sanctions or lift them entirely.

This false choice came out of a limited five-track engagement plan developed in mid-2016. This plan is insufficient, as Ambassador Lyman also noted, because it doesn't address basic governance issues in Sudan, doesn't include crucial human rights and religious freedom issues, and removes the bulk of U.S. leverage without requiring any peace agreement for the multiple wars being waged today in Sudan.

The far more sophisticated nature of the tools of financial pressure that are available today can be deployed in a much more nuanced way than sanctions on all of Sudan or no sanctions at all. Mr. Chairman, we believe Congress and the Trump administra- tion must correct this course and do so now by developing a delinked and independent human rights and peace track with the Government of Sudan that would supplement but remain independent of the five tracks.

This new track should focus on the United States' most pressing policy goals for Sudan: Advancing human rights, religious freedom, essential democratic reforms, good governance and, ultimately, a comprehensive peace.

Without addressing these goals, the Government of Sudan will maintain its longstanding patterns of behavior, advancing policies that have led to continuous deadly wars, religious persecution, dictatorship, mass migration to Europe, grand corruption, and affiliation with terrorist organizations that have marked its 28 years. Achieving the bold objectives in this new track will require tools that are more focused, sophisticated, and impactful than the dull instrument of comprehensive sanctions.

Instead, we must use state-of-the-art financial pressures that target key elements of the regime and the corporate and banking networks that underlie it. The comprehensive sanctions in place now come from a previous era and were, as was noted by Ambassador Lyman, never robustly implemented.

They nevertheless impacted the regime's ability to connect to the international financial system, especially in recent years, as sanctions enforcement triggered by a different program, Iran, caused global banks to review their systems and realize they were still banking Sudan through the correspondent banking network.

Rather than giving up on this renewed leverage now, Congress should adopt legislation that ties a new suite of modernized financial pressures as well as appropriate incentives to the new human rights and peace track.

The pressures we propose are not just a few more sanctions or variations on the broad measures of the past. It is a fundamentally different approach, shifting from one that is geography-based to one that is conduct-based and using both sanctions and anti-money-laundering measures.

In this new approach the measures would focus solely on individuals and entities that are responsible for major human rights abuse, grand corruption, religious persecution, conflict gold trading, weapons exporting, and undermining the peace process. These are the economic sectors that provide the regime its lifeline and the types of conduct that are most problematic.

So that is what we should target. Unlike the past, we should not just use the broadest of measures or try to pick a few names and never update them as they morph into new entities. We need to use the best financial intelligence available, which our initiative, The Sentry, will help provide, so as to achieve our foreign policy objectives and protect the integrity of the U.S. financial system.

For example, entities in Sudan like the National Intelligence and Security Service operate in ways not unlike entities the United States has targeted in Iran.

In addition, conflict-affected gold and weapons exports provide much needed off-budget cash that is used to sustain violence and line the pockets of corrupt elites who have transformed the Sudanese economy into a private domain for their own enrichment.

The United States knows now to target these kinds of systems. OFAC, FinCEN, and the State Department have done so in relation to Iran, Russia, and Burma, to name a few. We just need to be willing to do it with Sudan.

Taking this course would be in stark contrast to the five tracks, which I will address very briefly. As my colleague, Omer Ismail, recently described in testimony before the Lantos Commission, some of the violence in Sudan has eased, in part due to the evolving nature of the use of force in conflict areas, and we note that Sudan has demonstrated restraint with respect to South Sudan and likely continued its counterterrorism cooperation.

At the same time, as Omer and many others have testified, the restraint in some areas contrasts with continued violence in the conflict zones. There have been numerous violent attacks on civilians in Darfur.

Government fly-overs continue to threaten people in South Kordofan including the Nuba Mountains. Worse, while the Government of Sudan is allowing cross-border humanitarian access to areas in South Sudan affected by famine, parts of Blue Nile and South Kordofan remain restricted.

Acknowledging both progress in areas where the five-track plan benchmarks are unmet, we believe two things should happen. The interagency assessment process should continue and an honest assessment made in July.

Our expectation is that the five tracks will remain unfulfilled when viewed as an entire package because at least two of the five tracks will not be in compliance.

If the government is indeed noncompliant on any of the tracks, then the final step of complete removal of the comprehensive sanctions should be delayed for a sufficient period such as 1 year.

In addition, in response to the violence in Darfur and as a way of reinforcing the need for serious engagement on all five tracks leading up to July, the administration should use its authority under the Darfur sanctions, which are not part of this plan, to impose asset freezes on those responsible for the violence.

As with other sanctions programs connected to serious negotiations, the administration should tighten pressure along the way to reinforce those objectives while also providing relief.

In the end, the fate of the five-track plan and the comprehensive sanctions should be a lower priority because it creates a false policy choice—comprehensive sanctions or nothing over benchmarks that do not fundamentally alter the nature of a regime that has wrought havoc within Sudan and the region for nearly three decades.

Mr. Chairman, members of the subcommittee, Congress should take the lead in designing a clear U.S. policy approach, one that deploys the types of modernized pressures that can generate meaningful leverage for creating real and lasting change in Sudan through a human rights and peace track.

Thank you for the opportunity.

[The prepared statement of Mr. Brooks-Rubin follows:]

The project to end genocide and crimes against humanity

Testimony of Brad Brooks-Rubin
Policy Director to The Sentry and The Enough Project
House Foreign Affairs Committee, Subcommittee on Africa, Global Health, Global
Human Rights, and International Organizations
"The Questionable Case for Easing Sudan Sanctions"
April 26, 2017

Chairman Smith, Ranking Member Bass, Members of the Subcommittee, thank you for holding this important hearing and providing The Enough Project and our financial investigative initiative, The Sentry, with the opportunity to share our perspective on a country that has long vexed U.S. policymakers. Congress has a deep and bipartisan history of leading U.S. efforts to promote peace, human rights, religious freedom, and counterterrorism objectives in Sudan, and this is an absolutely critical moment for Congress to continue that engagement.

It is a critical moment because, this past January, in the waning moments of the last Administration, an all-or-nothing choice on economic sanctions on Sudan—either maintain the two decades-old comprehensive sanctions or lift them entirely—was created. This false choice came out of a limited, five-track engagement process that was developed in mid-2016. This process is insufficient because it does not address basic governance issues in Sudan, it does not include crucial human rights and religious freedom issues, and it removes the bulk of U.S. leverage without requiring any peace agreement for the multiple wars being waged today in Sudan. The far more sophisticated tools of financial pressure that are available today can be deployed in a much more nuanced way than a "sanctions on all of Sudan" or a "no sanctions at all" approach.

We believe Congress and the Trump Administration must correct this course—now. This correction can best be achieved by developing a de-linked and independent Human Rights and Peace Track with the Government of Sudan that would supplement but remain independent of the five-track engagement process. This diplomatic track should address the most critical reform issues in Sudan, and it should be tied directly to modernized and focused financial pressures tools, as well as new incentives, which can maximize the chances of achieving U.S. foreign policy objectives in Sudan.

This new track should focus on the United States' most pressing policy goals for Sudan: advancing human rights, religious freedom, essential democratic reforms, good governance, and ultimately a comprehensive peace. Without addressing these goals, the Government of Sudan will maintain its longstanding patterns of behavior, advancing policies that have led to the continuous deadly war, religious persecution, dictatorship, mass migration to Europe, grand corruption, and affiliation with terrorist organizations that have marked its rule for the last 28 years.

Achieving the objectives in this new track will require tools that are more focused, sophisticated, and impactful than the dull instruments of comprehensive sanctions we have previously used. Instead, we must use state-of-the-art financial pressures that target key elements of the regime and the corporate and banking networks that underlie it. The comprehensive sanctions in place now come from a previous era and were never robustly implemented and updated. But they nevertheless affected the regime's ability to connect to the international financial system, especially in recent years, as sanctions enforcement triggered by a different program—Iran's—caused global banks to go back, review their systems, and realize they were still banking with Sudan through the correspondent banking system. As banks then started to work harder to cut their ties to Sudan, the Government of Sudan launched an aggressive public relations and propaganda campaign, blaming U.S. sanctions for all the miseries inflicted on the Sudanese people by its own massive grand corruption and poor policies.

Rather than giving up this renewed leverage, Congress should adopt legislation that ties a new suite of these modernized financial pressures, as well as appropriate incentives, to a new Human Rights and Peace Track. In particular, the new pressures should include very specific and robust targeted sanctions based on the best financial intelligence available (which our initiative, The Sentry, will help provide) and anti-money laundering measures designed to achieve our foreign policy objectives, and more effectively protect the integrity of the U.S. financial system. This new track can also include incentives: if issues concerning Khartoum's relationships with terrorist groups not covered in the five-track engagement process are included here, the status of Sudan as a State Sponsor of Terrorism should also be under renewed consideration.

The financial pressures that should be associated with the Human Rights and Peace Track are not just a few more sanctions, or variations on the broad measures of the past. These pressures would constitute a fundamentally different approach, shifting from one that is geography-based to one that is conduct-based. In this new approach, the new pressures would focus solely on individuals and entities that are responsible for major human rights abuses, grand corruption, religious persecution, conflict gold trading, weapons exporting, and undermining any peace process. The approach targets those whose conduct drives this regime, and then it seeks to disrupt the facilitating corporate and banking network that supports them.

We must use the types of dynamic, modern approaches that were taken against Iran, Burma, and Russia and can address the corporate networks and economic sectors in Sudan that provide the financial lifeline to the Bashir regime and enable its repressive capacities and ability to inflict harm on Sudanese citizens. Entities in Sudan like the National Intelligence and Security Service (NISS) operate in ways that are not unlike the entities that the United States has targeted in Iran. In Sudan, conflict-affected gold and weapons exports provide much-needed, off-budget cash that is used to sustain violence and line the pockets of the corrupt elites who have transformed the Sudanese economy into a private domain for their own enrichment.

The United States knows how to target this kind of system; we just need to be willing to do it. Some of the key measures that we could take include:

- Sanctions that freeze the assets of Sudan's National Intelligence and Security Service (NISS) and its corporate network, establishing a 25 percent threshold for ownership that would result in designation.
- Sectoral sanctions focused on the conflict gold and weapons manufacturing sectors.
- Targeted sanctions on individuals responsible for acts of public corruption and serious human rights abuses throughout Sudan, ensuring we target individuals with significant personal assets and/or corporate holdings.
- Requiring compliance with these sanctions by foreign subsidiaries of U.S. companies to prevent evasion.
- Public reporting by companies doing business in Sudan in order to ensure companies are taking appropriate due diligence measures.
- Directing Treasury's Financial Crimes Enforcement Network (FinCEN) to investigate whether the gold sector or other networks in Sudan constitute a "primary money laundering concern," to issue advisories related to their investigations, and to work with financial institutions and other jurisdictions to investigate Sudanese Politically Exposed Persons and other targets. These efforts will focus the financial sector on the key concerns in Sudan and help to mitigate against future, large-scale de-risking.
- Congressional appropriation of funds to the relevant agencies to do this work that has been desperately needed for many years but never done.

These are the types of pressures, combined with appropriate incentives, that can generate meaningful leverage for creating real and lasting change in Sudan through the Human Rights and Peace Track. Changing the behavior of a genocidal regime requires use of the most effective tools we have at our disposal, tools that are narrowly targeted at the sectors and individuals most involved in committing mass atrocities against the population and diverting the country's rich resources to private purposes. By adopting this framework, Congress and the Trump Administration can finally implement a strategic approach to sanctions and pressures related to Sudan.

This approach would be in stark contrast to the five-track engagement process, which I will address briefly. As my colleague Omer Ismail recently described in his testimony before the Lantos Commission, some of the violence in Sudan has eased. We attribute this in part to the evolving nature of the use of force in the conflict areas. Nevertheless, there are parts of Sudan that have known a more peaceful period in recent months. We also note that Sudan has demonstrated restraint with respect to South Sudan, and we presume cooperation continues on many counterterrorism fronts.

At the same time, as Omer and many others have testified, the Sudanese government's restraint in some areas contrasts with its continued violence in the conflict zones. There have been numerous violent attacks on civilians in Darfur. Government fly-overs continue to threaten people in South Kordofan, including the Nuba Mountains. There were militia attacks in Blue Nile this year, and in the military campaigns it launched in 2016 the Sudanese government forces used a large quantity of new weapons and new types of military equipment, as Conflict Armament Research has documented. Worse, while the government of Sudan is allowing cross-border humanitarian access to areas in South Sudan affected by famine, humanitarian access for parts of Blue Nile and South Kordofan states remains restricted. The people in several isolated areas urgently need assistance and have been killed while moving through active conflict zones to find food and basic supplies.

Meanwhile, Sudan has used the provisional easing of the sanctions put in place in January, not to begin the necessary reforms of the structural deformities of the country's economy, but instead to order fighter jets and battle tanks from its traditional arms suppliers, Russia and China. These procurements, when concluded, will buttress the regime's preferred choice of settling internal conflicts by military means rather than through negotiated approaches that resolve the root causes of conflicts. These types of short-term purchases are made possible by easier access to financing in the global marketplace, principally because there are fewer concerns about the potential for single transactions in a specific timeframe to be blocked or rejected, and a generally more enabling economic environment within Sudan where there is more available capital.

Acknowledging both the progress and areas where benchmarks are unmet, we believe two things should happen with respect to the next steps of the five-track engagement process:

- The interagency assessment process should continue, and an honest assessment should be made in July. Our expectation is that the five-track engagement process will remain unfulfilled when viewed as an entire package, because at least two of the five tracks will not be in compliance. For example, if entire regions of Sudan remain off-limits for aid organizations because of Sudanese government restrictions, continuing this policy of using the denial of food as a weapon, should the United States really permanently remove its sanctions? That would certainly be a shocking outcome even to the architects of this five-track engagement process. If the government is indeed noncompliant on any of the tracks, then the final step of complete removal of the comprehensive sanctions should be delayed for a sufficient period, such as one year.

- In response to the violence in Darfur, and as a way of reinforcing the need for serious engagement on all five tracks leading up to July, the Administration should use its authority under Executive Order 13400, the Darfur sanctions—which are not part of the five-track engagement process—to impose asset freezes on those responsible for the violence. As with other sanctions programs connected to negotiation or engagement processes, the Administration should tighten pressure along the way to reinforce the objectives.

In the end, the fate of the five-track engagement process and the comprehensive sanctions should be a lower priority, because it creates a false policy choice (comprehensive sanctions versus nothing) over benchmarks that do not fundamentally alter the nature of a regime that has wrought havoc within Sudan and the region for nearly three decades. Congress should take the lead in designing a clear U.S. policy approach, one that deploys the types of modernized pressures that can generate meaningful leverage for creating real and lasting change in Sudan through a Human Rights and Peace Track. Changing the behavior of a genocidal regime requires use of the most effective tools we have at our disposal, which could narrowly target the individuals and entities that are most involved in committing mass atrocities against the population and diverting the country's rich resources to private purposes. We should ensure that these measures are tied to clear foreign policy objectives. This would give the U.S. government the best chance to effectively address its core policy objectives in Sudan.

Sudan Sanctions Background

As a reminder to the Committee, President Clinton imposed sweeping economic sanctions on Sudan in November 1997, highlighting the Bashir regime's support for international terrorism, destabilizing activity throughout the region, and human rights violations, particularly related to religious freedom and slavery.

These were comprehensive trade sanctions, not quite as sweeping as those for Cuba or Iran, but close. The sanctions prohibited all imports and exports of goods and services to or from Sudan, as well as new investment in Sudan, any transactions related to the petroleum or transportation sectors in Sudan, and so on. They also "blocked" and prohibited all transactions with the Government of Sudan, meaning that any such transactions would not only be prohibited, but also funds would be frozen if they came into a U.S. bank or into the hands of other U.S. persons. Targeted sanctions, where we name a specific person or company to a list and freeze their assets, had only begun to be used by the U.S. government as a tool in 1995, so this broad-brush approach was really all we had in the toolbox in 1997.

A second Sudan-related program, connected to Darfur, was imposed in 2006 and did use the targeted model, specifically to implement U.N. Security Council resolutions; this program has resulted in the sanctioning of a total of seven people and one company, with not one name added during the entirety of the Obama Administration. As with the Government of Sudan sanctions, should a U.S. person, such as a bank, have a transaction involving one of these eight targets, then it must freeze those funds.

To round out the picture, Sudan was named to the State Sponsor of Terrorism list in 1993, though this has much more impact on U.S. development assistance and diplomatic/international financial institution engagement than as a direct economic sanctions measure.

Throughout the 2000s, Congress passed several pieces of critical legislation—the Sudan Peace Act, the Darfur Peace and Accountability Act, the Sudan Accountability and Divestment Act of 2007 among them—and this legislation had a significant impact on Sudan policy, as well as easing sanctions in 2006 on certain parts of what is now South Sudan.

For the most part, these programs have remained in place in a more or less static form. The blunt, comprehensive sanctions remained in place largely unchanged for almost 20 years, with elements implemented by both the Departments of Treasury and Commerce. As such, the sanctions start to lose their effect because they are not tied to dynamic policy goals; sanctions that remain static for 20 years simply become policy unto themselves.

For example, only twice after the year 2000 did Treasury add any names to its sanctions list for these Government of Sudan sanctions, once in 2004 and once in 2007 as a response to the Darfur crisis. In both cases, the names added to the list were not even "new" sanctions. These were actions to identify companies or entities that were technically subject to sanctions already by virtue of being owned or controlled by the Government of Sudan, but where that may not have been clear to banks or the public. Perhaps needless to say, this is far, far fewer than the number of times Treasury acted to add names or identify blocked property in comparable comprehensive sanctions programs like those for Iran and Cuba.

The failures to develop or enforce the sanctions over two decades enabled the Bashir regime to create ways to go around the sanctions. There were—helpfully—steps taken to ease the impact of sanctions on the people of Sudan during the Obama Administration, although more could have been done in this regard as well. But throughout the last Administration, there was no demonstrable attempt to create greater leverage directly with the Government of Sudan or the worst actors in the regime, nor was there an effort to build on the sanctions mechanisms that were already in place.

In general, enforcement of Sudan sanctions through civil penalties lagged behind other comprehensive programs like those for Iran or Cuba, despite repeated promises by State and Treasury officials to step up enforcement efforts against violators, notably in 2007 in connection with efforts to address the Darfur crisis.[1] Sanctions without the willingness to conduct the necessary investigations and enforce actions against violators will not be effective against a resourceful regime that will find evasion methods, no matter how the sanctions program is crafted. Congressional leadership is essential to ensure the agencies administering and enforcing sanctions are well resourced and have the political direction necessary for them to be able to focus on a country like Sudan.

Over the last several years, however, sanctions did begin to take a stronger bite. Specifically, as Treasury, Justice, and the State of New York stepped up enforcement of sanctions against global banks, particularly for manipulation of the correspondent banking system, and as these enforcement actors imposed penalties in the hundreds of millions and even billions of dollars, the Government of Sudan saw some of its banking channels close. BNP Paribas, in particular, which prosecutors claimed played a central role in providing access to the U.S. financial system for the Government of Sudan, paid billions of dollars in penalties.[2]

Again, this was not enforcement originally intended to affect Sudan—it was focused on Iran and other threats—but it swept up Sudan because of the existence of comprehensive sanctions against the country. That is, as one bank after another started to receive these penalties, all major banks started to look at their own transactions and businesses and disclose (or receive subpoenas from the government requiring them to disclose) their own violations. They simultaneously began to look for ways to minimize risk, which meant examining correspondent and other relationships and ensuring that Sudan was excluded from their systems.

Of course—and this is an important consideration moving forward with the new Human Rights and Peace Track and related pressures—this process of working harder to ensure they had no connection to Sudan was largely driven by sanctions, but not entirely. Sudan's place for several years on the list of countries with deficiencies in its anti-money laundering system and its overall abysmal ranking as a place to do business also played into these decisions.

The Government of Sudan then began to feel the pinch and stepped up its propaganda campaign, arguing for how sanctions were hurting the Sudanese people—which is true in some cases. But as shown by a report released by the Enough Project yesterday, called *Sudan's Deep State*, the real damage to the people of Sudan comes from the Government of Sudan itself and its creation of a violent kleptocracy, including stealing from the people to benefit the corrupt inner circle of President Bashir, and using violence as a means of maintaining power while it manipulates key economic sectors, such as gold, weapons, and land. According to official figures, Sudan spends more than 70 percent of its annual budget on military and security, while spending less than 2 percent of the budget on health, education, and social services.

Five-Track Engagement Process and Sanctions Relief

Midway through 2016, the Obama Administration took the Government of Sudan up on what became Khartoum's principal pre-occupation: to stave off further enforcement and de-risking and have sanctions removed. To do so, the Administration created a five-track engagement process, focusing on a series of specific issues. These tracks cover important concerns, and the United States asked the Government of Sudan to make progress on each.[3]

There has been some progress achieved during the six-month implementation period, including the absence of a dry-season military offensive and an apparent reduction in Sudanese meddling in the war in South Sudan. However, six months is not enough time to gain confidence than any changes will endure, especially given the lack of independent verification mechanisms. As my colleague Omer Ismail recently testified before the Lantos Commission, echoing many other voices, the easing of violence is not necessarily a result of newfound Sudanese government restraint but rather "the evolving nature of the use of coercive force in the conflict areas." In addition, he noted that "there have also been significant attacks and other security incidents in South Kordofan (including in the Nuba Mountains) and in Blue Nile in the last nine months" and that access to urgently-needed humanitarian assistance has not improved in many areas. Overall, the Sudanese government continues to commit acts of violence, abuse human rights, and engage in corrupt activities.

More critically, the five tracks failed to address the internal pathologies in Sudan that perpetuate the system of violent kleptocracy developed over close to three decades. Three of the five tracks largely address regional issues. The tracks failed to incentivize opening of political space—for example, by freeing political prisoners or halting the practice of routinely closing down newspapers—or an inclusive political process in which Sudanese people from all groups can openly discuss the future of their country. This deficiency allowed the Khartoum regime to continue its relentless attacks on religious freedoms, free expression, and the rights to association and peaceful assembly, even as the regime technically complied with many of the benchmarks for the five tracks. The regime also forged ahead with a unilateral political process through a national dialogue that designed to impose a *fait accompli* on the opposition and the population and to further secure its grip on power.

Despite outlining a set of limited tracks and securing only initial progress on those limited tracks, the Obama Administration took steps to give away nearly all of the leverage it could use in future engagement, at least in the short or medium terms. This past January 13, mere days before President Obama left office, Treasury issued a General License that allowed U.S. persons to conduct all transactions that had been prohibited for years by the comprehensive sanctions. Imports, exports, financial services, investment, transactions with the Government of Sudan—all are now permitted.

Even more surprisingly, the United States unblocked more than $30 million, according to the most recently available Terrorist Assets Report,[4] in frozen funds and allowed them to be returned, a step normally reserved for the very end of a sanctions program.

Finally, on January 13, President Obama issued an Executive Order that set the clock ticking on a six-month process to determine if progress is maintained on the five tracks. If the interagency reports to the President that Sudan has maintained progress, the November 1997 Executive Order and other related orders will terminate, with sanctions ended. True, seven people and people company will remain subject to sanctions related to Darfur, and the State Sponsor of Terrorism designation will also remain in place, but nearly all the remaining potential for leverage and pressures to achieve a negotiated political solution, imperfect though they have been, will be terminated without attempting to use smarter or more modernized tools. The Executive Order created an all-or-nothing approach to sanctions—either the comprehensive sanctions or nothing—that was simply not necessary and not appropriate, given the limited nature of the five tracks.

That the negotiations on reform and some element of sanctions removal began is not the objection—that's always the goal of well-designed sanctions: to incentivize targets to change behavior in a manner that achieves a specific policy goal. But in this case, the design and execution were flawed, and the action taken is potentially disastrous, given that the Government of Sudan has already undertaken a public relations campaign touting the end of sanctions and is seeing some previously closed banking channels start to reopen. Given the many challenges of doing business in Sudan, it will certainly be some time before there is large-scale investment, but these are important steps to note.

Contrast this, briefly, with the U.S. Government's posture toward Iran, where many years of sanctions and pressures led to a negotiation on an important but particular subset of issues, with the lifting of a particular subset of the sanctions on the table. Regardless of your position on that agreement, there is general consensus that the pressures led the Iranians to negotiate. And it is notable that at every stage of that negotiation, the United States met progress from Iran not only with the prescribed limited relief but also with more pressure. In at least three instances in 2014 alone,[5] during the heart of the negotiations, in the days before or after key negotiation sessions, Treasury took sanctions measures, whether new designations or penalty cases. And when doing so, the Treasury press releases made the direct connection with the need for leverage in negotiations.

In sum, in general with Iran, the U.S. government tightened sanctions, got concessions from Iran, and kept tightening pressure at key moments to create leverage for the policy outcome it sought. Many certainly remain critical of the specifics and of the ultimate result, but the process itself was far stronger than that taken with Sudan. In the Sudan case, the U.S. government did not tighten sanctions, it got limited concessions, and it eased almost all sources of financial pressure, giving up much of its leverage for achieving its overall desired policy outcome. The different results reflect, at least in part, the contradictory approaches to sanctions.

Noting our many concerns with the five-track engagement process, if the Trump Administration decides to continue this approach, then it should ensure that an honest assessment is conducted to assess whether progress on these tracks is demonstrable and real, to ensure that all tracks are evaluated and verified, to ensure that no single track is unduly privileged over others, and to see that pressure is used to respond to violations. Specifically, we believe:

- The interagency assessment process should continue, and an honest assessment should be made in July. Our expectation is that the five tracks will remain unfulfilled when viewed as an entire package, and if that is the case, then the final step of complete removal of the comprehensive sanctions should be delayed for a sufficient period, such as one year.

- In response to the violence in Darfur, and as a way of reinforcing the need leading up to July for serious engagement on all five tracks, the Administration should use its authority under Executive Order 13400, the Darfur sanctions—which are not part of the five-track engagement process—to impose asset freezes on those responsible for the violence. As with other sanctions programs connected to negotiation or engagement processes, the Administration should tighten pressure along the way to reinforce the objectives.

A Human Rights and Peace Track, with Leverage

This approach is insufficient if we are seeking more fundamental change in Sudan, and Congress should work to make sure the Trump Administration changes it, through support, pressure, and legislation. As such, we focus instead on the most essential need—the need to launch an independent, de-linked Human Rights and Peace track to address the most pressing policy goals related to Sudan: ending the Bashir regime's use of violence, disrupting the corrupt networks and violent kleptocratic system that our report *Sudan's Deep State* documents in great detail, and bringing peace and genuine political reform to the country.

This track must encompass essential reforms concerning political space, human rights, religious freedom, and good governance. The United States must approach this Human Rights and Peace track with what it missed with the first five: dynamic and focused leverage that targets and enforces meaningful pressure on the most entrenched elements of the regime and targets its financial lifelines. This leverage must be precise, forceful, and consistent. When a commitment is made along the Human Rights and Peace track by the Bashir regime, which has so often broken its promises to the United States and the international community, the response should not be automatic easing in an all-or-nothing dynamic, but reinforcement of the pressure, along with necessary incentives, as a sign of the United States' seriousness of purpose. Build pressure, show results, and that approach will change the dynamic between the United States and Sudan over time.

To ensure this approach is deployed, Congress should introduce strong, bipartisan legislation that ensures that the strategy of negotiating this Human Rights and Peace track is coupled with appropriate incentives and necessary pressures that include elements detailed below, which go beyond sanctions to include anti-money laundering measures. In addition to appropriate incentives, these measures in particular can more forcefully and systematically target the proceeds of corruption being placed in the international financial system, often by transiting through New York, by requiring banks to focus on the conduct more than the specific individuals or entities involved:

Sanctions:
- In order to have an impact on one of the core elements of the regime's corrupt corporate footprint, authorization of sanctions on any companies owned or controlled by the Sudanese National Intelligence and Security Service (NISS) or any senior NISS officials. These sanctions should include:
  - Establishment of a requirement for ownership/control percentage threshold for sanctions at 25 percent, rather than 50 percent.
  - Creation of a "watch list" of companies that may not meet that threshold but require additional investigation.
- Authorization of sanctions for any individual or entity involved in weapons manufacturing or in the gold sector, the latter in order to combat the problem of

conflict-affected gold. These sanctions should also include the following elements in order to ensure compliance throughout the financial sector:
- o Foreign financial institutions providing financing for either the weapons sector or industrial gold mining may face denial of correspondent banking privileges or involvement in U.S. government contracts.
- o Prohibition on U.S. persons from any direct or indirect activity that results in the financing of these sectors.
- o Extension of these prohibitions to activities of foreign subsidiaries of U.S. companies.
- Authorization of sanctions on any person facilitating or benefiting from acts of public corruption or any person responsible for serious human rights abuses committed by the Government of Sudan.
- Requirement that companies doing business in Sudan grossing more than $100,000 should report to the U.S. Embassy in Sudan with criteria similar to the Burma Responsible Investment Reporting Requirements, which is supported by many large companies and ensures sufficient levels of due diligence.

Anti-money laundering:
- Require FinCEN to conduct an assessment of the Sudanese gold sector, including an identification of countries that import Sudanese gold, the entities involved, and the extent to which the gold sector is enriching the Government of Sudan.
- Require FinCEN to pursue issuance of an investigative request, pursuant to Section 314(a) of the Patriot Act, to financial institutions for records pertaining to Politically Exposed Persons, their corporate networks, and individuals and entities of concern with respect to the gold sector.
- FinCEN should report on its determination of whether any institutions, accounts, or classes of transactions within or related to Sudan should be considered a "primary money laundering concern" pursuant to Section 311 of the Patriot Act.
- Treasury and State should conduct (i) outreach to banks and financial institutions relating to preventing the processing of transactions on behalf of the regime or the Sudanese Politically Exposed Persons identified above, (ii) outreach to European, Asian and regional Financial Intelligence Units relating to anti-money laundering enforcement and investigations related to Sudan and Sudanese Politically Exposed Persons; (iii) outreach to banks and governments highlighting the need to continue processing transactions to benefit the Sudanese people.

Congress should also ensure that Treasury has sufficient resources to conduct the necessary investigations and then implement and enforce the actions taken.

Conclusion
Implementation of these smarter, more targeted sanctions and AML pressures, along with vigorous enforcement and integration with our negotiation strategy on, and incentives linked to, the most critical policy issues within Sudan, can raise the chances of success over the long term on the Human Rights and Peace track, which must be the policy focus.

Endnotes

---

[1] U.S. State Department, "Remarks on Darfur and Sanctions," John D. Negroponte, Deputy Secretary of State; Adam Szubin, Treasury Department Office of Foreign Assets Control Director; and Andrew Natsios, Special Envoy to Sudan, Washington, DC, May 29, 2007, available at https://2001-2009.state.gov/s/d/2007/85716.htm. ("The most important part of the President's announcement this morning in terms of the actual coercive measures are the enforcement mechanisms.")

[2] Nate Raymond, "BNP Paribas sentenced in $8.9 billion accord over sanctions violations," Reuters, May 1, 2015, available at http://www.reuters.com/article/us-bnp-paribas-settlement-sentencing-idUSKBN0NM41K20150501; United States of America v. BNP Paribas S.A., Statement of Facts, June 28, 2014, available at https://www.justice.gov/sites/default/files/opa/legacy/2014/06/30/statement-of-facts.pdf.

[3] The five tracks are (1) de-escalation of the violence in conflict areas; (2) improving humanitarian access to populations in need within these areas; (3) refraining from destabilizing the peace process in South Sudan; (4) cooperation in containing threats from the remnants of the Lord's Resistance Army (LRA); and (5) supporting the U.S. counterterrorism efforts.

[4] U.S. Treasury Department Office of Foreign Assets Control, "Terrorist Assets Report: Calendar Year 2015, Twenty-fourth Annual Report to the Congress on Assets in the United States Relating to Terrorist Countries and International Terrorism Program Designees" (Washington), available at https://www.treasury.gov/resource-center/sanctions/Programs/Documents/tar2015.pdf.

[5] U.S Treasury Department, "Treasury Designates Additional Individuals and Entities Under Iran-related Authorities," Press release, December 30, 2014, available at https://www.treasury.gov/press-center/press-releases/Pages/jl9731.aspx; U.S. Treasury Department, "Treasury Targets Networks Linked to Iran," Press release, August 29, 2014, available at https://www.treasury.gov/press-center/press-releases/Pages/jl2618.aspx; U.S. Treasury Department, "Treasury Targets Networks Linked To Iran," Press release, February 6, 2014, available at https://www.treasury.gov/press-center/press-releases/Pages/jl2287.aspx.

Mr. SMITH. Mr. Brooks-Rubin, thank you so much for your testimony, and Enough over the decades has been ever pressing for a better Sudan and I want to thank you for your insights today.

I would like, before we take a brief recess, to catch those three votes that are on the floor. We have been joined briefly by Dr. Oscar Biscet, one of the greatest human rights defenders in the world, who has spent years in the gulag in Cuba.

He was in solitary confinement many times. He's an OB/GYN, a medical doctor, and a group of us some years back nominated him for the Nobel Peace Prize because of his extraordinary work and his courage.

So I want to just acknowledge him and thank him for his leadership for so many, many years and now that he is free I would point out that he testified twice before our subcommittee. One time he did it after he was under house arrest.

He did it by way of phone hook-up at great risk to himself while he was still in Cuba and he testified before this subcommittee and made a very, very strong and powerful statement on behalf of human rights. Thank you, Doctor, for being here.

Again, I apologize to our two witnesses. We will come right back. It should only be about 15 minutes. Then we should have a big open time to get into Q and A. Thank you. Stand in recess.

[Recess.]

Mr. SMITH. The subcommittee will resume its hearing and Mr. Dettoni, I believe you're next.

Again, I apologize for the delay but we should be clear for the entire hearing now.

STATEMENT OF MR. DAVID DETTONI, SENIOR ADVISOR, SUDAN RELIEF FUND

Mr. DETTONI. Chairman Smith, Ranking Member Bass, other members of the subcommittee, I want to thank you for your long, long service on human rights in Africa.

Both of you, I know you've been very involved and your work here, as I wrote in my written testimony, your constituents may never know all the lives and the impact that you're making in the world and I just wanted to thank you for all the service that you're doing.

We've already mentioned or other people have already mentioned the five areas that are in the sanctions that the Obama administration temporarily lifted in January 2017, and I'm just going to run through those real quickly and then address my views on if those are a valid rationale and then try to focus on some recommendations for Congress and the Trump administration.

First, on the issue of enhancing cooperation on counterterrorism, I have to say I think that my view is probably simplistic and I know it's hard line, but the sins of Bashir and the regime, I just don't see how those sins can be forgiven.

They hosted al-Qaeda for several years. Attacks occurred on our Embassies in Tanzania and Kenya. Thousands of American lives have been ended because of Khartoum and Bashir's material support for terrorism, and this isn't even half the story on their support for terrorism.

They need to be held accountable. You said at the beginning of this hearing in your opening remarks you've held countless hearings on human rights, peace, I mean, coming on 15, 20 years.

And so when are they going to be held accountable for these acts? And it's not like it's just another dictatorship around the world. These are people who are still in power, some out of power, who are anti-American, anti-Western and they have—they have—their actions have had an impact that are diametrically opposed to the interests of this country.

So the first thing is, I know it's simplistic but I think that lifting the sanctions for cooperation on counterterrorism is not forgivable and I think that they need to be held accountable for their actions.

The nature of this regime in Khartoum is that they kill their own people. They kill their own citizens. They don't even blink when they do it.

They didn't blink when they were supporting terrorism or whatever they are still doing or not doing and they haven't blinked in killing women and children intentionally, particularly what I know about is in the Nuba Mountains, dropping bombs on schools, hospitals, churches.

I've seen them. There are holes in the roofs. Every school, every hut has a foxhole in it so that the children or the pastor or priest can run and hide into a foxhole.

I was going to try to bring in some shrapnel from these bombs that have exploded and that have killed innocent people, and I didn't want to bring it in because I didn't know if I'd be able to get it through and have the hassle of it.

But I've got them. Bombs drop and if you're not in a foxhole and you're within 100, 200 meters of this thing, it's going to spin hundreds of miles an hour and it's going to cut off your head, cut off your arm, go right through you.

That's the reality of what they are doing to their own people and that's the reality of the nature of this regime.

They are still in power, and I know it's a simplistic view but that's the reality of what they have been doing up until very recently and they can do again, and to their own citizens.

On the issue of humanitarian access, particularly in the two areas, to my knowledge, Khartoum has not allowed a single piece of humanitarian assistance into the two areas. People haven't planted crops like they would when there is peace and stability.

The people of Nuba have been attacked and invaded for over 6 years now, since 2011. It's a war zone. So there is little food. There is no development. There is no building for the future.

There are virtually no doctors. There is one surgeon in the Nuba Mountains. Woe to you if you get appendicitis and you can't reach Dr. Tom Catena, an American serving at Gidel Hospital.

The humanitarian situation, particularly in the two areas which I know about, is dire and it's part of Khartoum's strategy, just like it was in the war with South Sudan, to deny the two areas humanitarian assistance.

I will say this. I'll acknowledge one positive thing that I've seen Khartoum do and that is in an ironic twist they've allowed in South Sudanese, 100,000, 200,000 refugees, and they have a semblance of safety there. And as well, there are, I think, between

100,000 and 200,000 Eritreans who have fled the repressive regime in Eritrea.

Now, Khartoum's doing this because it's in their interest. I don't think they are doing it because they think it's the right thing to do.

But ascribing motives is neither here nor there, and the thing is, though, that they are, I think, using, particularly with the Eritrean issue, they are using us with the Europeans to stem the refugee flow and getting money and funding to keep the refugees in Sudan. So I think that they are gaining some benefit out of it as well.

In the past several months, hostilities in the two areas has been greatly reduced. The aerial bombing, to my knowledge, has ceased. No major offenses or skirmishes on any sort of scale have oc- curred and both sides—the major sides involved, Khartoum and the SPLM-North, have restrained. However, there is no formal cease-fire.

There are no mechanisms to enforce a cease-fire, no modalities, no observers except for maybe the United States with the sanctions that we have used as leverage, and the fighting and bombing can begin at a moment's notice.

The Comprehensive Peace Agreement, I need to touch on that be-cause we keep having hearings and talking about Sudan, particu-larly as it concerns the two areas. Khartoum did allow South Sudan to vote for independence. But on many other aspects of CPA they just clearly violated the Comprehensive Peace Agreement of 2005.

In May 2011, Khartoum invaded Abyei, destroying, killing, looting, displacing over 100,000 Dinka, who are indigenous to Abyei. And now there is an Ethiopian peacekeeping force that are preventing any further outbreaks, hopefully.

But that was a Khartoum—clear violation of the Comprehensive Peace Agreement and it included violence. The CPA provided for popular consultation for the two areas. The citizens of Abyei, as we know, were promised a referendum to decide which country they belong in.

That hasn't happened. But the CPA provided for popular con-sultation for the people of the two areas. That hasn't happened. In-stead, what happened?

In May 2011, Bashir gave the SPLM-North 1 week to disarm their army and my understanding is that CPA provided for 1 year to integrate security and get security arrangements figured out be-tween the SPLM-North and Khartoum. Instead, it was 1 week and then Bashir and his allies attacked and resumed the civil war, which has been going on within Khartoum and the two areas for almost 6 years now.

From personal experience, the CPA provided for political partici-pation and freedom of movement and assembly. When I was in Khartoum in 2011 when I was a staff member of the U.S. Commis-sion on International Religious Freedom, several members of the transitional government and National Assembly were marching in a peaceful protest on the steps of the assembly to present their problems and their issues with the way the government was going. As we were going out to the refugee camps, we saw thousands of Interior Ministry troops coming their way and we learned later that the security forces had arrested these National Assembly members, beaten them up, kicked them, and we saw the bruises and we saw the impact upon this.

And this was the beginning of the end of, to me in my mind, of implementation of the CPA, particularly as it regarded the two areas.

So what are my recommendations for the new administration and for Congress? First, President Trump needs to appoint a high-level Special Envoy for Sudan and South Sudan.

This person needs to have direct access to President Trump. The appointing ceremony should occur in the Rose Garden. President Trump should conduct a press conference.

In his remarks he should note the expectation that the Special Envoy should travel to the Nuba Mountains, the two areas, Khartoum, Darfur, Juba, South Sudan, and Sudan.

To my knowledge—correct me if I am wrong, Ambassador Lyman, no Special Envoy has ever traveled to the two areas to see for themselves the situation on the ground.

I believe they've gone to Khartoum. They have never gone to the two areas. This needs to change. Second, the Trump administration needs to reset relations with South Sudan.

As a signatory to the CPA and as a major stakeholder in the creation of South Sudan, the United States has a moral obligation to help the South move off the precipice of total collapse and President Trump having a personal relationship with President Salva Kiir might help to improve the conditions in South Sudan and the region.

Despite being two independent countries, Sudan and South Sudan's futures are linked. The solutions to both political and civil war crises must be found and it's in our, America's, strategic and moral interest to bring peace and stability to the region and to these two countries.

Third, within 6 months of today, President Trump should hold a regional conference in Washington, DC, and invite and have a have attend President Salva Kiir, the President of Uganda, the President of Kenya, the Prime Minister of Ethiopia and maybe a few others.

Promote a unified agenda for peace, democracy, stability and security in the region and finding unified approaches to the problems in Sudan and South Sudan.

Fourth, working with Congress, President Trump should either amend the January 2017 Executive order lifting some sanctions or ask Congress—the President should ask Congress to draft legislation, or you should just draft it on your own, concerning sanctions on Sudan.

President Trump, or legislation, should make a lifting of sanctions reviewable every 180 days or annually, as was suggested earlier, and there should be a requirement the executive branch must submit to Congress in writing and to the President a rationale review for action on sanctions toward Sudan.

Such a review should be publicly viewable 2 months before the sanctions should be lifted and it should be written such that the sanctions are not automatically lifted if the President doesn't take action, like they are right now.

These sanctions, my understanding, will be automatically lifted unless the President revokes them or does something to them. The stoppage in the fighting in the two areas has been a positive development and needs to be sustained and a sustained lull can create an environment and a situation more conducive to lasting peace.

Now, a basic question is why Khartoum has to do something in their own interest in the sense of making a peace deal and ceasing to fight and kill its own people.

But if a few select sanctions can be waived 180 days or a year and it keeps the fighting down and they are negotiated in good interest I think it's worth trying.

Fifth, the chairman of the full committee, the ranking member, the chairman, other members, should request a classified briefing from relevant agencies on Sudan's counterterrorism assistance to the United States.

In that same briefing, the agencies should provide a report detailing the involvement of Khartoum and the extent of Khartoum's meddling and past activity and present activity in South Sudan and the region.

After receiving this briefing then you could ask those agencies to give the same briefing to other members of the committee and other Members in the Senate and the Congress.

I want to give President Trump and his team an opportunity to build on the fact that the fighting in the two areas has ceased and the fighting can begin at a moment's notice.

The region is waiting to see how President Trump will lead and the new Congress will lead and amend, change direction or build upon the work from previous administrations.

We want to give President Trump the ability to lead in this volatile region and my belief that—of limiting the lifting for a little bit of time could lead to a certain transparent, reviewable and certifiable process that involves the Congress and congressional approval and might provide leverage and better behavior from Khartoum.

My hope is for the President to become personally engaged in the peace process in the Sudans and for the President to develop a personal relationship with our allies in the region.

I believe it's in the interests of the United States. I believe it's in the security interests of the United States to use the resources and leverage of American power to promote peace, prosperity, and freedom in this troubled region.

Thank you.

[The prepared statement of Mr. Dettoni follows:]

Written Statement of David Dettoni, Director of Operations, Sudan Relief Fund

House Committee on Foreign Affairs, Subcommittee on Africa, Global Health, Global Human
Rights, and International Organizations, The Questionable Case for Easing Sudan Sanctions;
Wednesday, April 26, 2017, 2:30 p.m.

I want to begin by thanking Chairman Smith, Ranking Member Bass, and the Distinguished
Members of the Subcommittee for your public service and valuable work exercising oversight
into American policy towards the wide range of extremely important issues under this
Subcommittee's jurisdiction.

Many of your constituents may not understand how your work on this Subcommittee affects
them in their daily lives, but your oversight, intervention, and attention to American policy
related to Africa, Global Health, Human Rights, and International Organizations, saves lives and
makes a difference in the world. Furthermore, when America has neglected Africa, human
rights, and global health, we have done so at our peril or great tragedies have occurred.

An example of a great tragedy that occurred in the areas under this Subcommittee's jurisdiction
was the slaughter of millions in Rwanda over the course of weeks while America basically sat on
the sidelines. While the genocide in Rwanda did not pose an existential security threat to
America, it did pose an existential threat as to the type of country we, the United States are and
who we aspire to be as a people. The United States cannot be the world's policeman, but there
are moral crises which arise which if we as the United States neglect, fail to respond, or fail to
anticipate, America's neglect of these crises, past and future, will have the effect of decaying our
great nation. In turn that moral decay will affect our children and our children's children, until at
some point, we don't recognize our aspirations and our foundations as a country. My former
boss and former colleague of yours, Congressman Frank Wolf, used to incessantly repeat the
Biblical imperative: to much whom is given, much is required. America has been given much
and therefore much is required.

What are some examples of American neglect in Africa leading to peril? Al Qaeda claimed
responsibility for killing over 224 people—Americans, Kenyans, Tanzanians-- when our
Embassies in Kenya and Tanzania were blown up in 1998. More to the subject at hand, Al
Qaeda was likely able to accomplish these attacks and many others, including the bombing on
9/11 because Al Qaeda moved its headquarters to Khartoum, Sudan at the invitation of Sudan's
Omar Bashir and his accomplices with the National Islamic Front/National Congress Party. This
is the cadre of militant Islamic jihadists who seized power in Sudan in a coup in 1989 and who I
believe have not relinquished their power or Islamic based, Anti-American, Anti-Western
ideology in the parts of Sudan that they control.

For this hearing, I have been asked to discuss my observations of the situation on the ground in
Sudan and whether or not I believe they justify the proposed easing of sanctions that President
Obama lifted a week before his eight years of service ended as President of the United States.
Certainly in the background of all of my comments on the conditions justifying or not justifying
the lifting of sanctions for Sudan is this lingering issue: The current leader of Sudan, Omar
Bashir, and the cadre of power in Khartoum provided material support for attacks against
America that killed thousands of Americans. The ideology and politics of current political
leaders and the cadre in Khartoum, more often than not, have been diametrically opposed to
American interests.

One of the traits I admire about our country, the United States of America, is how we have befriended and become allies with so many of our former enemies. I believe this is a pragmatic trait of Americans and our former leaders, meaning it is in our interests to become allies with our former adversaries, and it is also because I believe we Americans fundamentally want to help the world become a better, safer place for all people. Germany and Japan are now two of our closest allies. We fought for independence from Great Britain and then fought again, and now they are very close allies.

In the case of Sudan, the same cast of characters, the same power base that promotes a perverted and violent expression of Islam is still in power. Look at Sudan's "President". It is still Omar Bashir. The same man who invited Al Qaeda to live in his hometown and set up a headquarters, to establish training bases, to recruit Sudanese to kill Americans. He and his power base are still intact and I do not think their fundamental belief system has changed, meaning, what drove them to power and drove their political and social agenda was a perverted and distorted version of Islam, a version that a vast majority of devout Muslims around the world most certainly reject and find abhorrent.

America, in contrast to Khartoum, is not a theocracy, and our policy makers do not have to embrace a religious dictum such as "all sins must be forgiven". For me, Khartoum's likely continued embrace of a corrupt religious ideology that promotes violence and hate and the fact that this same regime and political actors was ground zero for Al Qaeda operations and recruitment, is an unforgivable sin.

The Obama Administration's justifications for lifting sanctions announced on a publicly released fact sheet on January 13, 2017, by the Office of the Spokesperson for the Department of State, listed five reasons for justifying lifting the sanctions which included, ceasing hostilities in Darfur and the Two Areas, improving humanitarian access, ending negative interference in South Sudan, and addressing the threat of the Lord's Resistance Army (LRA), and enhancing cooperation on counterterrorism,.

On Sudan "enhancing cooperation on counter terrorism", I've read many public reports of how this cadre of power in Khartoum began to cooperate with the United States and our allies on issues of terrorism after the attacks of 9/11. Reportedly, many in the security profession were pleased with the information and other assistance received. I cannot judge the helpfulness of the counter terrorism cooperation, but it seems counterintuitive to reward the same group of people who promulgated and allowed the terrorism in the first place. Not only do they get some type of reward, they are allowed to continue to be in power.

As you Members on this committee realize, policy decisions are not always a choice between two good options, sometimes policy decisions are choices between evils, or to put it another way, policy makers are faced with making decisions that are less than ideal.

Sudan's supposed enhanced cooperation on "terrorism" does not come without a price. The events of 9/11 and Al Qaeda's attacks against American in Africa and around the world, are more distant. The supposed "junior varsity" team of DAESH has shown its capabilities and atrocities, and they and Assad, Hezbollah, and Iran seem to be center stage in the Middle East. I hope America and our allies are safer, and that lives and tragedy have been saved because of the supposed counter terrorism cooperation. Nevertheless, I believe some actions by rulers are unforgivable and that linking the lifting of sanctions to a regime that has not fundamentally changed its leaders, outlook and fundamental political beliefs, is not justified.

I have been asked to comment on whether I believe the sanctions being lifted are justified based on conditions on the ground in Sudan and I will direct the rest of my comments towards what I know to be conditions on the ground with a more specific focus on the Two Areas, whether Khartoum has improved humanitarian access, how the cadre in Khartoum implemented the Comprehensive Peace Agreement of 2005, and Khartoum's ending its negative interference in South Sudan.

On the issue of humanitarian access, according to UNHCR, since 2013 Khartoum has allowed some 380,000 refugees from the chaos and civil war in South Sudan. My understanding is that humanitarian access to all of these camps is controlled, and monitored by Khartoum's security services and that refugees do not have freedom of movement around the rest of Sudan. I've heard life is tough in these camps, but Sudan has allowed these very vulnerable and suffering people to have a form of refuge. The cadre in Khartoum has also allowed perhaps 200,000 Eritrean refugees to have refuge in Sudan. These poor Eritreans presence in Sudan probably gives a form of sanctuary to them that is better than their suffering in Eritrea.

However, Khartoum seems very effective in using their supposed benevolence as leverage for political or other goals that they want to achieve. The Enough Project has just published a report titled *Border Control from Hell: How the EU's migration partnership legitimizes Sudan's "militia state"*, that describes how the European Union is improving relations with Khartoum as a basis to stem the flow of refugees into Europe, providing millions of Euro for equipment and training efforts to Sudanese security type forces to decrease or stop the flow of illegal migration to Europe. Sudan has been known as a transit and collection point for the flow of illegal migration to Europe. I was surprised to learn from a European official whose daily job is to work on refugee issues, that Eritrean refugees are particularly not wanted in Europe as they have very few job and foreign language skills, they are poorly educated, and many have psychological trauma from forced conscription in the Eritrean military. The cadre in Khartoum is shrewd. They are using the refugee and illegal migration crisis to their advantage, using their "humanitarian efforts" to loosen sanctions, gain respect, gain valuable foreign currency. As long as Bashir and his cadre are in power, America should never forget who we are dealing with in Khartoum, nor what they and their cadre did to America.

On the issue of humanitarian access to the "Two Areas", South Kordofan/Nuba Mountains and Blue Nile State, I do not believe any humanitarian access has crossed the battle lines from Khartoum into the two areas. Since the implosion of the Comprehensive Peace Agreement, the only type of "assistance" Khartoum has brought to the Nuba Mountains and Blue Nile is military, and the guns, tanks, rockets, aerial bombardment is not meant to develop or grow individuals, but to maim, destroy, kill. I suspect many of us who have remotely followed Sudan issues for the past many years can become numb to the constant fighting, with some new military movement or disagreement arising every few years. Whenever I visit the region, I am struck by the fact that Bashir and his cadre, are intentionally killing their own people. Thousand pound bombs with Cyrillic handwriting drop from Sudan Air Force planes to kill women and children tilling their fields. Innocent children lose their limbs when shrapnel from their "government" tears them apart.

I have been on the ground in the Nuba Mountains when Khartoum's Antonov bombers circled over me, and a few hours later, visited the burning huts and the crying, grieving parents of a child who had just been slaughtered by Bashir's weapons that he and his cronies use against the innocent citizens of Sudan. We cannot ever forget that Bashir and his supporters in Khartoum are killing their own people in cold blood to achieve their political and religious objectives.

Humanitarian conditions in the Two Areas is dire. Planting and harvesting of food has not occurred on any scale as people are concerned about the resumption of hostilities at any time. Food is scarce. Malnutrition is rampant. There are virtually no doctors in the Nuba Mountains. Almost no one is available to give basic life-saving surgery to those in need except for an American citizen named Dr. Tom Catena who faithfully conducts surgery in the Nuba Mountains. Child birth deaths are outrageously high. Women suffer and die giving birth or from complications. No building or development is occurring as people cannot get material to build, and they are worried about any structure being bombed or targeted by Khartoum. Khartoum has attacked by air or ground any structure it can see, churches, schools, hospitals. Churches and schools have foxholes scattered around their buildings so the children and worshippers can flee to safety feet way from where they worship or learn. I have seen the destruction of churches, school classrooms that are flattened by Khartoum's bombs. What kind of supposed government intentionally drops bombs on its own children while they are at school???

In terms of assessing Khartoum's abiding by the Comprehensive Peace Agreement of 2005 signed with the Sudan People's Liberation Movement (SPLM), Khartoum has abjectly failed in implementing this agreement as it concerns the Two Areas and with the Sudan People's Liberation Movement North. Khartoum did allow the South to vote for independence, but the cadre in Khartoum violated most of the other key aspects to the agreement regarding the oil rich disputed area of Abyei, and against the Northern element of the SPLM, the SPLM North (SPLMN).

The Abyei region sits between Sudan and South Sudan and is claimed by both countries. The CPA determined that the residents of Abyei were to vote in a referendum held simultaneously as the referendum on the independence of South Sudan in January 2011. Khartoum insisted that a nomadic pastoralist tribe that historically grazed its cattle for a few months a year, the Misseriya, should be determined as residents of Abyei. South Sudan insisted that only the year round residents, the Ngok Dinka, should be counted as residents. In May 2011, Khartoum invaded Abyei, burning, looting, destroying, killing and forcing the removal of over 100,000 Ngok Dinka. South Sudan and Khartoum negotiated that Khartoum forces would depart Abyei and a UN mandated force of Ethiopian peacekeepers has been on the ground in Abyei subsequently to this day. The referendum on Abyei has still not occurred, but Khartoum's invasion of Abyei was a very clear and violent breaking of the Comprehensive Peace Agreement.

Unlike the supposed referendum for Abyei that has still not occurred, the CPA provided for a "popular consultation" to ascertain the views of the people of the Two Areas. The popular consultation has not occurred. Instead, Bashir and the cadre in Khartoum gave the SPLMN one week notice, in May 2011, to disarm, in violation of the CPA. My understanding of the CPA is that it provided for one year for the SPLMN and Khartoum to negotiate a new security agreement and integration of units if the people of South Sudan chose for independence, which of course, we all know the people of South Sudan voted for independence. Bashir and his cadre in Khartoum began to forcibly disarm the army of the SPLMN triggering the resumption of the civil war between the Two Area and Bashir/Khartoum. This was another clear violation of the CPA by Bashir and his cadre.

The CPA recognized the freedom of assembly and provided for political participation and representation in the Transitional Government of Sudan that was comprised of the ruling cadre of Bashir/Khartoum and the SPLM AND SPLMN. I was in Khartoum in 2009 on an official U.S. delegation with the United States Commission on International Religious Freedom. Several members of the National Assembly allied with the SPLM tried to peacefully walk to the steps of the National Assembly in Khartoum to present a list of grievances of violations of the CPA by Bashir and his supporters. As our delegation drove we witnessed thousands of Interior Ministry troops driving into the city center and we later met with the SPLM Members of the Parliament who had led the march and learned they had been detained, kicked and beaten with batons by Bashir's security forces. This was a clear violation of the CPA and it signaled the beginning of the end of Bashir's implementation of the CPA as it applied to the Two Areas, and political participation of political parties not aligned with Bashir.

Lastly, the Obama Administration listed "progress over the past six months" , on the issue of Khartoum ceasing its negative interference in South Sudan and that the lifting of some U.S. sanctions has been used as leverage in all of the various areas in which the Obama Administration outlined. Exactly what "negative influence" specifically means was not described in the published press release or subsequent announcements. Bashir's security apparatus was well known during the war with the South for supporting various splinter or disaffected Southern rebel groups to fight or cause trouble against Dr. John Garang's led factions and the main SPLM. Bashir's security forces know perhaps better than anyone else in the world how to fuel instability and chaos in South Sudan, given that it was part of their war strategy for decades against the SPLM. I believe Khartoum and Bashir are partly to blame for the chaos and killing that has occurred since South Sudan gained independence. The South Sudanese generals, political leaders and others are not blameless, so all of the guilt is not on Bashir, but certainly, Bashir and his security forces have not contributed much to stability or the strengthening of South Sudan. Riek Machar and other Southern warlords received material and other support from Khartoum during the long civil war with the SPLM and my eyebrows certainly were raised when in the past few years, Khartoum gave Riek Machar sanctuary after the major conflagration between Machar and other elements of the ruling Southern SPLM party. Indeed, Machar announced a resumption of military fighting from a pulpit in Khartoum after he arrived. Machar quickly left Khartoum after he made this announcement, and to my knowledge has not been allowed back, so presumably, Khartoum no longer perceived it in their interests to allow Machar to make pronouncements of war from the streets of Omdurman. Whether Bashir and Khartoum have made progress over the past year on ceasing their negative influence on South Sudan is very difficult to know unless one has access to classified intelligence. I believe before the Obama Administration entered into discussions with Bashir and his cadre, Sudan most certainly was quite a disruptive and negative player in South Sudan, fueling the crisis and massive humanitarian situation in South Sudan.

So, what should the Trump Administration's position be in regards to President Obama's Executive Order issued January 13, 2017 revoking some U.S. sanctions on Sudan? What should Congress do in response to the January 13, 2017 Executive Order?

I believe the Trump Administration has until July 12, 2017 either to revoke or amend President Obama's January 13, 2017 Executive Order or it will come into effect. This means that the Trump Administration has a little more than two months to review the pertinent issues and decide how to act. One option is that President Trump can do nothing which means some specific sanctions are lifted permanently. Another option is for President Trump to revoke all or parts of President Obamas January 13 Executive Order.

My recommendations are the following.

First, President Trump needs to appoint a high-level Special Envoy for Sudan and South Sudan. This person needs to have direct access to President Trump. The appointment ceremony should occur in the Rose Garden and President Trump should conduct the press conference. This needs to occur in the next few weeks, or as soon as possible. In President Trump's remarks, he should note his expectation that the Special Envoy should travel to the Nuba Mountains, the Two Areas, Khartoum, Darfur, Juba, other areas in South Sudan, and Sudan. To my knowledge, no Special Envoy from the United States has ever travelled to the Two Areas to see for themselves the situation on the ground. This needs to change.

Second, the Trump Administration needs to do a reset in relations to South Sudan. As a signatory to the CPA, and as a major stakeholder in the creation of the newest country in the world, the United States has a moral obligation to help move South Sudan off the precipice of total collapse and President Trump having a personal relationship with President Salva Kiir might help improve conditions in South Sudan and the region and encourage peace and stability. Despite their being two independent countries, Sudan and South Sudan's future and prosperity are linked together, and solutions to both political and civil war crises must be found and it is in America's strategic and moral interests to bring peace and viable solutions.

Third, within six months from today, President Trump should hold a regional peace conference in Washington, DC and meet with South Sudan President Salva Kiir, President of Uganda Yowero Musveni, the President of Kenya, Prime Minister of Ethiopia Hailemariam Desalegn, others, to promote a unified agenda for peace, democracy, security assistance, and stability in the region and in finding unified approaches to the problems in Sudan and South Sudan.

Fourth, working with Congress, President Trump should either amend President Obama's January 13, 2017 Executive Order or ask Congress to draft legislation concerning sanctions on Sudan. An amended Executive Order by President Trump or legislation from Congress should make the lifting of some or fewer of the sanctions listed in President Obama's January 13, 2017, reviewable every 180 days or annually. The Executive Order should contain a requirement that the Executive Branch must submit in writing to Congress and to the President a rationale and review for action on sanctions toward Sudan. Such a review should be as publicly viewable as is possible and should be submitted to Congress and to the President 2 months before the sanctions could be lifted. The Executive Order should be written such that the sanctions being conditionally lifted are not automatically lifted due to Executive inaction, requiring the Executive Branch to prove that progress is being made along certain areas or the sanctions will be automatically revoked.

The stoppage in fighting in the Two Areas has been a positive development and it needs to be sustained. Both the SPLMN and Bashir have mostly kept the fighting to a minimum. The sustained lull in fighting can create an environment and situation more conducive to a lasting resolution to the conflict between the SPLMN and the cadre in Khartoum. It begs the question as to the true nature of Khartoum if it needs some type of sanctions to be lifted for it to act in the interests of its own citizens and people. Lives are at stake. I would like to see the people of the Two Areas live more in peace. At the top of the list for a new Special Envoy for Sudan and South Sudan must be to establish a more formal cease fire in the Two Areas and to establish modalities for humanitarian assistance to be delivered, without Khartoum having the ability to control or deny access to such assistance. The people in Khartoum have not been subjected to daily aerial bombardment, nor with facing sustained, intensive invasions, but I also hope for the average citizen in Khartoum and its environs, to have the benefits of sustained peace.

Fifth, Chairman Royce, Ranking Member Engel, Chairman Smith, Ranking Member Bass, the Majority and Minority leadership of the House, and the appropriate counterparts in the Senate should request a classified briefing from the relevant U.S. agencies on Sudan's counter terrorism assistance to the United States. In that same briefing, the agencies should provide a report detailing the involvement and extent of Khartoum's meddling and negative influence in South Sudan and the region, detailing current and past activity with specific dates involved. After receiving this briefing, and determining its merit, Mr. Smith and Ms. Bass could ask the agencies to provide the briefing to other Members of Congress.

Sixth, President Trump should issue an Executive Order immediately amending President Obama's January 13, 2017 Executive Order on sanctions, and require the Secretary of State, to provide the report hitherto required to be provided to the President on or before July 12, 2017, to be provided to the President, and the Congress, on or before June 12, 2017.

In conclusion, I do not believe Bashir and the cadre in Khartoum's actions of material support for terrorism against the United States should be forgiven and those in and out of power in Khartoum need to be held accountable for their actions against the United States.

Bashir and the cadre in Khartoum have broken the CPA with impunity and they need to be held accountable for this, not rewarded. Bashir invaded Abyei and his forces looted, killed, raped and stole from the indigenous tribe that lives there year round. The regime in Khartoum violated the CPA in invading the Two Areas, demanding the SPLMN to disarm in a week.

Bashir and the cadre in Khartoum certainly bear some responsibility for the chaos and instability in South Sudan. They should not be rewarded so quickly for possibly ceasing to be such a negative, malicious actor.

That there has been minimal fighting in the Two Areas over the past several months is a fact. I believe that the offer of some sanctions against Sudan being lifted, may have contributed to the cease fire in the Two Areas.

I want to give President Trump and his team an opportunity to build on the fact that the fighting in the Two Areas has mostly ceased. The fighting in the Two Areas can begin again, at a moment's notice, and I believe the region, and the leadership in the region is waiting to see how President Trump will lead, amend, change direction, or build upon the work from previous U.S. Administrations.

We want to give President Trump the ability to lead on Sudan and South Sudan, and in this volatile region in Africa. I believe my recommendations on limiting the lifting of some sanctions against Sudan to a certain, transparent, reviewable and certifiable process that also involves Congressional approval could provide America with leverage and encourage better behavior from Bashir and Khartoum.

My hope is for President Trump to become personally engaged in the peace process in Sudan and South Sudan, for President Trump to develop a personal relationship with our allies in Africa and with those African leaders who want him and America to succeed. I believe it is in the security interests of the United States and the region for Mr. Trump to help use the resources and levers of American power to promote peace and prosperity in this troubled region of Africa.

―――――

Mr. SMITH. Thank you very much for your testimony, recommendations, and for going there so frequently to be a first-hand witness. Thank you.

Mr. Abubakr.

STATEMENT OF MR. MOHAMED ABUBAKR, PRESIDENT, THE AFRICAN MIDDLE EASTERN LEADERSHIP PROJECT

Mr. ABUBAKR. Ranking Member Bass and members of the subcommittee, thank you for affording me the honor to testify before you today and to share my personal observations regarding the impact of sanctions on the ground in Sudan.

My goal is to provide you with evidence that you need to act. You have statistics and you have social aggregate data and you have——

Mr. SMITH. If you could just suspend for 1 minute and I apologize for the rudeness of it. But Mr. Garrett does have to leave I believe to meet with the Japanese Ambassador but really wanted to just express a few thoughts and maybe ask a question and then we'll go right back and take as much time as you want.

Mr. GARRETT. Sure, and I apologize specifically to you, Mr. Abubakr, because I'd love to—I need to hear what you say. I'm going to take the testimony and notes back with me.

This is a very important subject to me by virtue of some of the activities that we've engaged in that we alluded to earlier as it relates to the release of some prisoners currently held in the Republic of Sudan.

And I really want to also tip my hat to you, Mr. Dettoni, Mr. Brooks-Rubin as well, Ambassador. Your boss is Frank Wolf, or your former boss, is a really fine man who I think served Virginia and our Nation very well and it was my honor to count him among a distant circle of friends.

What I heard here, and I would welcome the input of anyone, what I wanted—maybe I heard what I wanted to hear. My efforts reaching out to the Embassy, the Ambassador and the Republic of Sudan's delegation here in the United States have been, obviously, with a clearly articulated goal and that is to win the freedom of these individuals and even if it means that they leave the nation.

We've obviously engaged in a relatively one-size-fits-all series of sanctions and certainly for well-articulated reasons here today. The question that I have is, and I think you touched on this toward the end of your testimony, if we might not be well advised to try to find that carrot as opposed to the stick, even in very limited measures.

What I've seen in my very micro-interaction is a desire for an improvement in relations, a willingness to be accommodating as it relates to moving in directions I think we would all find desirable where they feel it's in Sudanese interests, right.

And I understand human nature is motivated by I'm willing to do this if it's the right thing to do and there's something in it that helps me and my nation. I think I've seen that and I hope—obviously, President Bashir has been there for a long time and, certainly, for 11 years in one iteration and since, I guess, 1989 as President.

But with the cessation of active hostilities and certainly the dialogue that I have heard that the good-faith comments that have been made to me might it not make sense to slowly start to roll back sanctions and see if we don't see commensurate continued behavior?

I understand the history and certainly Darfur is something that the world can't turn a blind eye to. What does that mean in the Nuba Mountain region we don't even know.

But might it not make some sense to try to sort of give a little to see if we can get something that's in everyone's collective best interest? And Mr. Brooks-Rubin, you, I think, are moving to speak.

Mr. BROOKS-RUBIN. Thank you, Representative Garrett.

I think your point is well taken. I think the important issue to note is that that's—in some ways that's a five-track process that's been put on the table.

The comprehensive sanctions and the five-track process, unless it's completely amended and tossed aside, and we are recognizing that that process is underway, when that is completed at whatever point, and those tracks should be honestly assessed, but at whatever point that happens the comprehensive sanctions that are in place now being lifted, that's a significant carrot.

That is a significant development. That takes away all of the restrictions that are in place now with respect to imports, ex- ports——

Mr. GARRETT. I'm not trying to be rude. My understanding is that we anticipate the lifting of the sanctions based on the actions of the previous administration if the current administration agrees to it and that's all up in the air.

What I think Mr. Dettoni, and I'm not trying to argue with you because I think we're on the same page here, suggested is if this is done in a sort of progressive step-by-step fashion it's—let me paraphrase a better political figure than myself, trust but verify—that if we give to the Sudanese things helpful to the Sudanese and continue to do so so long as they behave in a manner such that we find to be more consistent with the spirit of human rights, then everybody wins, right?

My experience, in a vacuum, has been wonderful. But I know there's a whole lot bigger world out there.

Mr. BROOKS-RUBIN. Yes, I——

Mr. GARRETT. But it was an all or nothing, more or less, right?

Mr. BROOKS-RUBIN. Correct.

Mr. GARRETT. The previous administration said this is what we are going to do. We are on a 6-month clock right now.

Mr. BROOKS-RUBIN. It's all or nothing in terms of the sanctions for what is a limited set of actions by the government. I think what we are—what all of us are saying in different ways is we need to get the important issues, the key issues of peace, human rights, religious freedom on the table and then let's—that's what we need real incentives for and there are other incentives that are still on the table, as Ambassador Lyman noted, with respect to debt relief and State Sponsored of Terrorism.

But our view is if you're going to put really the rest of the issues on the table, those core issues of human rights and religious freedom, that can't just be without pressure.

There also need to be a different level of pressure to get there and so it's a different idea around what those sticks are. The stick we have now is a big blunt club from 20 years ago.

Mr. GARRETT. Right.

Mr. BROOKS-RUBIN. Let's come in with more precision-guided tools that can get there.

Mr. GARRETT. And so we say show me and what I've heard is, and again, I am looking at a tiny little slice—we want to show you. And I think—if I can build on that for a moment—if you look at the—certainly, there are self-inflicted causes for your famine in the South Sudan but if you look at infrastructure and who has access to the Red Sea and ports, et cetera, and rail facilities, albeit ones in dire need of some maybe U.S. assistance if everything goes well, it would help us to have a good relationship with the Sudan to get the food to the places that don't have——

Mr. SMITH. If you could just, out of respect for Mr. Abubakr. I know you have that——

Mr. GARRETT. Yes, sir. And I apologize to Mr. Abubakr.

Mr. SMITH. And I would ask all of you to circle back to the questions, and they are great questions, that Mr. Garrett has asked. But we'll maybe complete Mr. Abubakr's testimony, then come back——

Mr. GARRETT. Well——

Mr. SMITH [continuing]. Because I know you have answers to these questions.

Mr. GARRETT. But I guess if the Sudan plays ball, to use a colloquialism, it would be in the best interests of the entire region by virtue of just the ability to distribute food, et cetera.

Mr. SMITH. I think it——

Mr. GARRETT. You can nod——

Mr. SMITH. Okay. Go ahead.

Mr. GARRETT [continuing]. Shake your head no.

Mr. DETTONI. I don't want to be—I don't want to interrupt, Mr. Chairman, and you haven't spoken so maybe we can talk in private about this, not on the record.

Mr. GARRETT. I would invite you, anybody at the table to reach out to our office. I would love to speak with you, and I apologize, Mr. Chairman.

Mr. SMITH. And for the record, come back and answer those.

Mr. DETTONI. Sure. Sure.

Mr. SMITH. Mr. Abubakr. Thank you.

Mr. GARRETT. Thank you. I am sorry.

Mr. ABUBAKR. My goal is to provide you with evidence that you need to act. You have statistics and you have social aggregated data and you have political knowledge.

What I want to give you is my story. My name is Mohamed Abubakr, civil and human rights activist from Khartoum, Sudan, born and raised.

Inspired by the Universal Declaration of Human Rights, I've done the best I could to be there for those deprived of these rights the most, at an early age too, as Sudan has that tendency to force children to grow up way before they should, I grew up and spent most of my adult life in a comprehensively sanctioned Sudan.

It wasn't an easy experience by any means. As a citizen I struggled and as a student I suffered. The unintended consequences of sanctions that plagued the program put a heavy load on the average citizen of Sudan and an even heavier load on the back of civil society in Sudan and, specifically, on those of us in the humanitarian and human rights sectors.

Despite the exceptions made for organizations working in this space, while I personally have been outspoken about these unintended consequences and joined the calls for reformation and modernization of the U.S. sanction policy, I did not for a second doubt the importance of having them in place, or the rationale for their imposition. It wasn't hard to notice the strong correlation between the regime's financial comfort and violence.

So against many of our personal interests, citizens and civil society, we supported the sanctions. We believed they were about bringing positive change and transformation of the human rights scene in Sudan, and holding on to the hope for the light at the end of the tunnel we fully complied and fully backed the sanctions.

So you can imagine the deep sense of sadness and betrayal widely shared by many upon hearing about the U.S. intentions to ease sanctions and on these conditions—conditions that completely ignored the human rights and for the citizens of Sudan who suffered in silence for so long.

In my written statement, I argued against the rationale for easing sanctions against Sudan and whether sanction relief was warranted to begin with, and I argued against each of the conditions set forth by the U.S. Government for the easing of sanctions.

I argued against the legitimacy of Sudan as a partner in the war against the Lord's Resistance Army and its methods while the Government of Sudan and affiliated militia are still engaged in recruitment of children in the exact same fashion.

And I argued against Sudan being a part of the solution to the South Sudan crisis as that situation in that violent kleptocracy needs a serious international long commitment in building South Sudan's nonexistent institutions.

But none of that is as important as what I am about to say. After the European Union recently dropped the ball on its commitment for human rights by striking an ethically and morally questionable deal to stop the African refugees and economic migrants hailing from Africa to reach Europe and hired the very same Janjaweed militia that killed hundreds of thousands of people in Darfur, now rebranded as the Rapid Response Force, there is absolutely no other champion left in the corner of those of us in Sudan fighting for human rights and dignity for the human of Sudan.

The flame of hope is fading away and the way I see it it's up to the United States and up to this committee to keep that flame alive.

I see my time is running up and allow me to close my remarks for this.

Mr. SMITH. Don't rush it.

Mr. ABUBAKR. In the process of thinking what to do with Sudan and thinking of what conditions could have been better for sanctions relief, please put yourselves in the uncomfortable shoes of an activist for human rights or a journalist who dared to speak truth to power, one of the thousands and thousands unlawfully arrested, tortured, and worse.

Think of what would make things better for them and others like them. Think of me and the thoughts coming through my head right now and the scenarios and the very plausible scenarios playing in my head as we speak about the consequences of me coming here today, for me and for people I care about and love back home.

It certainly would have been nice if the conditions for sanctions relief included language that would make me feel a little less worried and a little more at ease.

Thank you so much.

[The prepared statement of Mr. Abubakr follows:]

Mohamed Abubakr
President, The African Middle Eastern Leadership Project

House Foreign Affairs Committee
Subcommittee on Africa, Global Health, Global Human Rights, and
International Organizations

April 26, 2017

"The Questionable Case for Easing Sudan Sanctions"

Chairman Smith, ranking member Bass, and members of the committee, thank you for affording me the honor to testify before you today, and to share my personal observations regarding the concrete impact on the ground in Sudan of U.S. sanctions policy. My name is Mohamed Abubakr. I am a Khartoum-born human and civil rights activist, and I am the President and founder of the African Middle Eastern Leadership Project (AMEL – Arabic for "hope"). AMEL is an organization that works to mobilize, empower, and unite millennial leaders and activists from the Middle East and Africa to build resilient, inclusive societies that are free from discrimination, persecution, and violent coercion, and to advocate for policies in support of these goals.

My goal is to share what I observed and experienced in Sudan, in hopes that it helps inform and advance the United States' efforts to constrain state-sponsored violence and promote space for civil society. I hope to help you see what I have seen and experienced so that we may all act to best effect change with a shared sense of the realities on the ground. So today, I will not repeat statistics and deep concerns about political figures that are already in evidence; rather, I will share with you my story about the impact of sanctions — because I have lived it.

Living Under Sudan Sanctions:

For most of my life, I have lived in a comprehensively-sanctioned Sudan. Having spent half a lifetime trying to protect and empower the vulnerable, and to prevent conflict, I respect deeply the impulse behind the sanctions that the U.S. and others have imposed on Sudan. They are principled sanctions, thoroughly vetted, I am sure, by foreign policy and economic experts. These experts make a persuasive case for such sanctions.

I hope to offer a complementary perspective from the ground in Sudan. I can attest that the sanctions have contributed to great reduction in government violence. Limited access to funds limited scale and sophistication of violence, as evidenced by the scaleback of operations in South Sudan in the late nineties. At the same time, sanctions on the Sudan government also have had unintended effects on Sudan's everyday citizens and struggling civil society, sometimes with devastating consequences. These consequences may not be immediately visible from to you from Washington, but on the ground they are very palpable--and at times severe--to the people of Sudan.

For example, until recently, Sudan's civil society has been practically unable to access or benefit from American content, online and offline, including educational and scientific resources. Sudanese citizens often could not purchase basic electronics, even when abroad. Many banks and professional organizations have so feared running afoul of the OFAC sanctions that they often simply refused to fund, do business with or engage with any individual or entity in Sudan.

Such unintended consequences have had an injurious effect on Sudan's civil society and human rights communities, to which I can attest personally. With banks fearing fines, humanitarian exceptions that were made for Sudanese NGOs in U.S. policy were not realized in practice. Moreover, the tough regulations disincentivized important U.S.-based organizations from providing essential financial support to deserving Sudanese human rights and humanitarian organization, and made it exceptionally challenging for civil groups to make use of modern online crowdsourcing programs to fundraise and become self-sustaining.

Civil Society Support for U.S. Sanctions

While I personally have been outspoken about these unintended consequences, and joined the call to revise, **modernize**, and reform the U.S sanctions regime, I do not doubt the rationale for their imposition. I, like most people in Sudan, also understand and appreciate that **the sanctions have significantly limited the ability of the regime to perpetuate violence**. And I, like many in the Sudanese civil society and human rights community, also believe that a sanctions policy with teeth -- even one with serious unintended impacts on civilians and civil society -- is still better than allowing the government of Sudan to access more funds to build their deadly security arsenals and militias.

The Sudanese people, and in particular the Sudanese human rights community, understand very well why each layer of sanction was put in place, and what it was intended to accomplish. We fully complied with and supported them despite our concerns and against many of our personal interests, out of belief in the good intentions behind them, and stronger-still belief that the sanctions were indeed limiting atrocities in Sudan. It wasn't hard to notice the strong correlation between the government's access to funds, and the escalation of its violence.

Civil Society's Response to Easing Sanctions:

One can therefore imagine the frustration Sudanese civil society and human rights leaders felt upon hearing that the United States would ease the sanctions, as opposed to revising and modernizing them. I would be less than candid if I did not alert this Committee to the sense of sadness and betrayal that we felt. **This concern**

was exacerbated by the conditions tied to the sanctions relief, which made no demands on the government to address the daily violations of human rights, the suppression of the press, and the unlawful arrest and torture of activists and journalists. Such easing of sanctions without requiring any reforms in exchange hurts the very people that the sanctions were created to protect.

The patience and resilience of Sudanese civilians and civil society was encouraged by the belief that the United States had created layered sanctions to address a range of crimes committed by the government of Sudan against its own people.

Challenges with Rationale Behind Sanctions Easing

The United States government's five-part public rationale for then dropping these sanctions was to help *"cease hostilities in Darfur and the Two Areas, improve humanitarian access, end negative interference in South Sudan, enhance cooperation on counterterrorism, and address the threat of the Lord's Resistance Army (LRA)."* An examination of each of these reasons, however, raises important practical questions about what the Sudanese government has done, or ever will do, to deserve such relief.

Firstly, with regard to the hostilities in Darfur, the government of Sudan has in fact done nothing to improve the situation in Darfur. On the ground, the regime has not taken any proactive steps toward reconciliation with the rebels in Darfur, and it is still conducting air bombardments of the Nuba Mountains region, where civilians are essentially helpless against such attacks. The Sudan government may currently not be further escalating the fighting, but it most certainly has taken no steps to cease hostilities.

Secondly, the government of Sudan has taken no action whatsoever to improve humanitarian access to rebel-held areas, nor has it granted any previously-blocked international humanitarian organizations access to war-torn areas since the sanctions relief was announced.

Thirdly, the narrative that the Government of Sudan is, or can be, part of the solution to the South Sudan humanitarian disaster does not reflect the reality on the ground. While the government wants to position itself as a key player to resolving the South Sudan catastrophe, this is a quintessential case of the fox wanting to protect the henhouse. Positive change in South Sudan needs serious, long-term intervention and investment in building its institutions and unifying its broken pieces, through an internationally supervised transitional justice and reconciliation process. And those efforts must be clear-eyed about the Sudan government and others' competing interests in the region. Anything short of that will fail.

Fourthly, the belief that sanctions relief would induce Sudan to cut off its terrorist ties to Iran and Hamas is based on the misguided assumption that renewed Sudan-Iran or Sudan-Hamas relations is even possible at this time. To get U.S. sanctions relief, the government of Sudan made the risky gamble of **irreparably** destroying its relations with Iran and joining the Sunni-lead assault operation in Yemen. This was a move that not only puts the regime in a vulnerable place of reliance on the Sunni powers, but also cuts off its weapons-trade activities with Hamas, which provided the Sudan government with significant income and leverage.

Sudan's great risk in irreparably cutting ties to Hamas, and Iran, and casting its lot with Sunni powers also yielded it great rewards. Regional Sunni powers and their allies worked on the Sudanese regime's behalf and called loudly for sanctions relief, thus amplifying the Sudan government's diplomatic propaganda campaign. The U.S. and others' **fears that Sudan might now reestablish relations with Iran are unfounded and misguided, in my view;** Iran is extremely unlikely to be interested in relations with Sudan after its very public expressions of animosity and proven unreliability. Moreover, **Sudan cannot easily re-engage in weapons-trade with Hamas**, given the border scrutiny imposed by Egypt, tight Israeli-Egyptian supervision of the Sinai, and without Iran to foot the bill. Sudan's support of Hamas was incentivized solely by financial benefits that are no longer available.

Finally, it is tragically ironic that the United States has legitimized the Government of Sudan as a partner in efforts to address the threat of the Lord's Resistance Army (LRA), and specifically its recruitment of child soldiers, while **child soldiers are recruited everyday by militias associated with Sudan's government, in exactly the same fashion as the LRA**. It is quite common to see children as young as ten years old holding machine guns in conflict areas dominated by the Sudan government's forces and militias. To collaborate with the Sudan government against the travesty of the LRA's child soldier recruitment practices, while overlooking that government's use of the very same tactics, undermines the very human rights policy changes that sanctions relief seeks to promote.

I believe that the United States instituted these sanctions relief criteria with an exaggerated sense of the GOS' credibility and commitment to improve human rights conditions, and of its will, capacity and leverage to combat extremism and brutality in the region. Under the current conditions set forward for sanctions relief, very little has actually been demanded of the government in return, and no meaningful progress has been delivered. Meanwhile, the people of Sudan see no post-easing change to give hope for improvements in their human rights. They now believe that they have been left behind by the United States and other international allies, and that these former allies have chosen to defend neither their own core values, nor the most vulnerable people in Sudan. They see too that the Sudan government has delivered nothing of lasting value to the United States.

Virtually No Change in Behavior:

Meanwhile, Sudan remains as engaged as ever in the very same activities that provoked the imposition of sanctions in the first place. While sanctions may have hurt the Sudan government's access to financial resources, and thereby reduced violence somewhat, their intentions have not changed. Sudan still harbors terrorist groups, homegrown and foreign, and daily violations of human rights of millions of people across Sudan are still mandated by government laws and enforced by its brutal security arsenal.

Sudan's much-feared National Intelligence and Security Services agency (NISS) is still engaged, with complete impunity, in activities that violate the Geneva Convention on a daily basis. The NISS continues to break international law -- it arrests and tortures political and social activists, civil society figures, and journalists. Peaceful protesters are shot dead in cold blood over and over again across Sudan, and anyone who expresses an opinion that may remotely disagree with the regime is a target. Large-scale human rights violations can be observed pervasively in Darfur, the Blue Nile states, and in broad swaths of the Kordofan region.

The military, and the other militias affiliated with the government, have continued to commit mass rape as a weapon of war with impunity in Darfur, as they have since the start of the war. Human Rights Watch reported in 2015 that *"Sudanese army forces raped more than 200 women and girls in an organized attack on the north Darfur town of Tabit in October 2014."* This is not an isolated case, and the lack of reporting about other such atrocities is due simply to the Government's concerted effort to prevent human rights organizations from accessing conflict-affected areas. As a Sudanese, I hear directly about what is going on from those who have seen it.

Finally, according to Amnesty International, chemical weapons were recently used against unarmed civilians. An Amnesty International report from September 2016 reported that *"using satellite imagery, more than 200 in-depth interviews with survivors and expert analysis of dozens of appalling images showing babies and young children with terrible injuries, Amnesty's investigation indicates that at least 30 likely chemical attacks have taken place in the Jebel Marra area of Darfur since January 2016. The most recent was on 9 September 2016."* Furthermore, the report stated that *"[t]he scale and brutality of these attacks is hard to put into words. The images and videos we have seen in the course of our research are truly shocking."*

No Remorse:

And yet, Sudan's President Al-Bashir shows no remorse for the brutality of his regime. In his last public address before sanctions-easing was announced, President Al-Bashir called the United States "**the land of the enemy.**" He did so after threatening the activists who lead peaceful civil disobedience against his policies, promising to do to them what he did in 2013. In 2013, his forces shot dead hundreds of peaceful protesters who took to the streets to protest the poverty and underdevelopment caused by the corruption and endless looting of Sudan's resources by Bashir's kleptocracy. Some of the dead were people I knew personally; I could easily have been one of them.

And in Bashir's first public address after the U.S. announced plans to ease sanctions, he bragged that the United States had failed to twist his hand, and eventually had given up and decided instead to shake it. He proudly **thanked Saudi**

Arabia and Gulf states for lobbying on his behalf in recent months because "**they recognized his regime was innocent, and unfairly treated.**" He showed no remorse, admitted no wrongdoing, and evidenced no willingness to change.

Europe's Bargain with Brutality

In fairness, the United States was far from alone in re-engaging Sudan with no demand for improvement in the human rights of our fellow humans in Sudan. Even worse, the EU engaged in morally-questionable activities that may themselves qualify as violations of human rights. The Sudanese people have been treated to the terribly sad spectacle of the European Union agreeing to pay Sudanese government forces to prevent Sub-Saharan and East African migration, including asylum seekers, from reaching the shores of Europe - at any cost. These government forces, today known as the Rapid Support Force (RSF), were created out of the Janjaweed Militia, the very same militia that the world watched kill hundreds of thousands of Darfurian civilians. Rather than punish the Janjaweed, the European Union has hired them. And the cost, especially for those forcibly returned to states they had fled, was indeed high.

With the European Union having sacrificed its commitment to human rights principles in return for an ethically-questionable and hopelessly-flawed deal, **the United States represents the Sudanese people's last and only hope.** If the United States goes down the same path as Europe; if this country, and this subcommittee, lets sanctions against the Sudanese government be significantly eased or removed without meaningful, tangible, and lasting improvement in Sudan's respect for human rights, it will drive a nail in the coffin of the Sudanese people's lingering dreams for a better tomorrow. Tragically, the nail in the coffin is likely to be real for members of the principled opposition in Sudan.

Conclusion

Respectfully, I urge that the United States further revamp its sanctions on Sudan as quickly as possible. This can be done in ways that restrain the most dangerous impulses of the Government of Sudan while opening space for the evolution of a civil society that helps to make the country, and the region, more stable and peaceful. I am one of many who will happily try to offer helpful input. The United States is the only standing ally for those who fight for human rights and liberal democratic values in Sudan. The members of this Committee, the government of the United States, and the many Americans across the political spectrum, as practical champions for human rights in Sudan are the last hope for the people of Sudan.

There are many ways to mitigate the unintended consequences on the people of Sudan as a result of U.S. sanctions, without giving what will, in my view, be an unrequited carrot to a brutal and unreliable regime. I have participated in many Sudan policy discussions with American civil society organizations, including the ENOUGH project, Humanity United, The National Endowment for Democracy and Human Rights Watch, and sanctions always take center stage in these discussions.

We have exchanged ideas and perspectives on sanction models that can achieve the intended results, even more effectively and without the counterproductive impacts that have plagued Sudan.

I am confident that this Committee, if it chooses to use its enormous power and intellect, can achieve a U.S. approach to Sudan that advances both near-term U.S. security objectives while also enhancing the deep unmet needs of the people of Sudan for liberty and dignity. And if you do, those people will, I assure you, fight hard to prevent and defeat extremism and brutality, and to create a more peaceful and prosperous society.

When evaluating the grim statistics and images of people suffering in Sudan, please picture those people as friends or family members, because that is who they are for me. Imagine hearing Al Bashir's ever- threatening words as if you were a surviving family member of the hundreds of thousands who perished in Darfur. Please try to put yourself in the shoes of an activist arrested and tortured for preaching human rights, or demanding democratic reform. Think, not of the data about the numbers of women gang raped and now raising the children of their rapists in Tabit and IDP camps, but of what it would mean to know, to have grown up with, to see, or god forbid to be, these women...

Think not in the abstract of a generation of Sudanese women and men that grew up in a comprehensively sanctioned Sudan, clinging to the hope and promise of light at the end of the tunnel, but of your human family. Then please, I ask, think about whether it is fair to them, or to U.S. interests, to reward a regime that as we speak is prosecuting multiple, major wars in Sudan, shutting down free speech, and regularly exercising brutal abuse of the human and civil rights of their own very vulnerable people -- men, women, children alike. ...

I also urge you to think carefully about what this sanctions-relief signals, both to the Al-Bashirs of the world, and to human rights defenders and those fighting for liberal democratic reform, in Sudan and the world. The choice doesn't have to be between pragmatism and idealism. United States interests can be served without military intervention on the one hand, or signaling the approval of such a regime on the other, but by instituting policies that empower those human rights voices on the ground to take control of their own destiny.

Which policies and which strategies will empower these voices, and which will block them from pursuing their values - values that you, in the U.S., share? What policies will bolster chances for peace and lasting friendship with the United States and its allies? I can testify, as one of these voices, that respectfully I believe that easing sanctions against the Government of Sudan will be a detriment to peace and human rights, and I hope you will consider my evidence.

Mr. SMITH. Thank you.

Ms. Bass.

Ms. BASS. Well, let me thank all of you for your testimony today and also for your patience.

I wanted to get a sense from maybe Mr. Brooks-Rubin when the Obama administration was determined to ease sanctions. If you could talk about the benchmarks that they saw. In other words, we are going to back up a little bit and this is what we expect to see from Khartoum. And then from Mr. Abubakr, you were describing what life is like with sanctions and maybe you could pose some alternatives; if we continue along the direction we are how do we get the regime to move?

Mr. ABUBAKR. I absolutely encourage reengagement with Sudan. It is not something that I'm opposed to, essentially. I really don't think the comprehensive sanctions is the way to go and that complete boycott is the way to induce any change.

I do believe, though, the modernized sanctions model put forth by the Enough Project could be a very effective way to go and reengage with Sudan.

I also believe when and if sanctions relief is warranted it should be completely human rights-based as that's, I think, in my opinion, the way to get to any other interest of the United States in the long term.

Reengaging right now on these sanctions, I'm afraid, will just leave the humans of Sudan behind for the very long run and I'm afraid nothing will ever change should these sanctions be removed on these conditions.

Ms. BASS. Thank you.

Mr. Brooks-Rubin.

Mr. BROOKS-RUBIN. Thank you, Representative Bass, and I think those are the issues that in some ways we would want to see in benchmarks for any comprehensive listing of sanctions is addressing exactly the issues that Mohamed and the other witnesses have testified to.

I think the issues with the five-track plan were that there weren't clearly established benchmarks. You had five tracks that were laid out, obviously, on counterterrorism. That's something that is, unless the classified briefing is held that Mr. Dettoni referred to for you, this is not something that anyone's going to have an insight into.

As to the other tracks, the Executive order says that progress needs to continue. But that's not defined, and in terms of understanding from the interagency what they're looking for, it's still an amorphous sense.

So understanding what continued progress on cessation of hostilities or humanitarian access is leaves too much to the eye of the beholder and this is a regime and these are issues that cannot be subjectively evaluated in exchange for a much larger peace.

If we had established sanctions relief that was measured, some small piece of the existing sanctions regime in exchange for some progress on these benchmarks, then there may have been a different discussion.

But you ended up with limited pieces of the issues mostly regionally focused, questionable progress on at least two of them, in exchange for what is at least the entirety of the economic sanctions program administered by the Treasury Department.

Without benchmarks, without clear steps that need to be met, it is impossible, really, for others to engage and really assess that well, which is, I think, why many are calling for this extension, at least on the five-track plan.

But from our perspective, wherever that five-track plan ends up, really, what's important are the big piece human rights issues that all of us have focused on here. That needs a much different set of benchmarks and a much different set of pressures as a result.

Ms. BASS. Ambassador, do you have a viewpoint on this?

Ambassador LYMAN. I fully agree, as I said in the testimony that what's missing in these benchmarks is the focus on some of the fundamental political issues including and especially human rights, et cetera, and that has to be the focus of the next round of discussion, because if you just only stick with these they're holding positions but they're not definitive.

But then one has to define what those steps are. What are the steps that you think are both feasible and meaningful? I think there are a number in terms of political for a space of stop harassing civil society and arresting people and torturing them.

There's a lot you can do in that area. It doesn't still answer the question of a political dialogue that ends the fundamental problems of the outlying areas. But one can make some very specific criteria in that area that at least starts to give space, and then one has to deal with both the other—some of the others.

So I think that is the key to the next round. But it doesn't wait until we get to July. In other words, that should be already part of the dialogue that's going on now so that regardless of how you come out in July you already have an understanding and agreement as to where this is going next.

If you don't have an understanding on that by the time we get to July, you haven't accomplished a great deal and so I think that has to start now.

Ms. BASS. Mr. Dettoni.

Mr. DETTONI. Well, Congressman Garrett said trust but verify. I can't allow myself to trust. I mean, given the history, all the broken agreements that have occurred, I can't allow—and I don't think we should have as a policy to trust Khartoum and its current regime.

Ms. BASS. What do you think should be done?

Mr. DETTONI. Well, I do think we need to tie the sanctions conditionally. I think the Trump administration needs more time to get their personnel in.

I think that they have been slow to put their people in and the administration needs to own this.

Ms. BASS. So you think they should put the sanctions back, the ones that were——

Mr. DETTONI. No. They should—we should extend the sanctions for 180 days or even a year because, yes, they have violated almost every agreement to a degree that they've made with the CPA.

They did allow the South to secede. There is a semblance of peace and there is some hope, I think, in the two areas in particular and I think that the new administration and the Congress needs to try to give this some life.

Ambassador Lyman can speak to this—there was almost an agreement on humanitarian aid. The Obama administration pushed very hard for an agreement in the two areas for the delivery of humanitarian assistance and I think it was just too much too late, and I think that the people who would not agree with it saw a new administration on the horizon and said, we just got to wait and see and we'll deal with the new administration.

So, give the administration some more time. Find these areas. Get their people in. The administration—they need to own it because it's—whatever happens in the region it's on their watch now.

Ms. BASS. Mr. Brooks-Rubin, I know in the Enough Project, and I think you made reference to—it's the Sentry? Is that what it's called? And I wanted to know if you could speak about that in terms of assets that you think are offshore.

Mr. BROOKS-RUBIN. Thank you, Representative Bass.

Yes, the Sentry is an investigative initiative that the Enough Project and other partners have launched to get at the question of if we are going to use all these policy tools we need to have the intelligence behind it to know who those targets are and who they should be.

So with respect to South Sudan, we've been able to document quite a lot of the properties of—and corporate holdings of the officials that are leading to that crisis and with respect to Sudan, the same.

So there are properties and assets that we are investigating around the region, and in other regions and we've looked extensively also at the banking network and trying to understand how— as I referenced in the testimony, how the Government of Sudan even during the sanctions was able to establish banking relationships that allowed correspondents—that allowed money to move and ultimately even move through New York through that system. So trying to understand where those banking nodes are will allow FinCEN at the Treasury Department or at other financial intelligence units and banks to zero in on where that money is moving and how they can stop it.

Even if the sanctions were to go away, in many cases what you're talking about are assets that are the proceeds of corruption. They are stolen from the people.

As that money moves through the financial system, banks can still go after it. The financial intelligence units can still go after it because it's money laundering.

The last thing I would say on the assets is looking extensively at gold. We have a report that we just issued yesterday called "Sudan's Deep State" that looks at the gold sector, the weapons sector, the land sector, and looking at how these sectors enable the regime and key leaders, key officials close to President Bashir, key entities I mentioned in my testimony, the NISS, an extensive corporate network that is enabling key members of the regime to move money around. That's where we can focus our tools.

So with the Sentry's information provided to the relevant actors, the hope is then they can take and use these kinds of financial pressures we have used to get at other regimes. We need to be able to do that for Sudan.

We need to be able to do that for the people of Sudan, to target those economic sectors and those actors and move away from this blunt instrument we had in the past.

But you need the information for it. We saw with the Sentry that there aren't a lot of the resources devoted to gathering this kind of financial intelligence around east and central Africa.

We, the U.S. Government, devoted to lots of other parts of the world. It's needed for east and central Africa and then the Sentry was the ability to say well, we can collect as much as we can—we'll turn that evidence over and then hopefully, use will be made of it.

Mr. SMITH. Thank you. Let me ask a number of questions and then take the ones you would like.

Mr. Brooks-Rubin, you, in your testimony, pointed out that Sudan has used the provisional easing of the sanctions put in place in January not to begin the necessary reforms of structural deformities of the country's economy but instead order fighter jets and battle tanks from its traditional arms suppliers in Russia and China.

Do you all agree with that? If you could elaborate on that. Let me just point out that with the Iran deal, which I thought was egregiously flawed on multiple fronts including the procurement and development of nuclear weapons and the means to deliver them in Iran, sanctions should have been allowed to stay in place far longer to get a deal that was verifiable and real rather than allowing them, minimally, after 10 years to have an industrial state capacity to produce fissile material.

Well, human rights were deliberately left out of that negotiation and the same thing happened with North Korea. We had Andrew Natsios, our former USAID Administrator and a man who wore many hats within previous administrations and an expert who also heads up a North Korea human rights organization, testified and he said there, too, in North Korea human rights are just thrown under the bus. No comments. Just work on the nuclear issue, and when that didn't materialize then no progress was made.

Matter of fact, just the opposite. They do have nuclear capabilities now and they're ever perfecting the means to deliver them. Human rights were unaddressed and now we have these five different mutually reinforcing areas where human rights are deemphasized, to put it mildly.

So if you could speak to the issue of what they're buying and, of course, what is Iran buying, like, perhaps Sudan—weapons, surface to air missiles in the case of Iran.

You point out that fighter jets and battle tanks are being bought. That, to me, would be a gross exploitation of the easing of sanctions.

Let me ask you, who's in charge? Bashir wanted to go to Turkey and the European Union asked Erdogan to arrest him and send him to The Hague, pursuant to the ICC indictment. And yet, he's travelled some 74 times over the years, although he did not go to Indonesia because several countries would not allow overlight airspace traversing by his aircraft.

So that put the kibosh on that. But China had him there, as we know, and others have as well—South Africa as well, and there's a court case.

Is he in charge? Maybe you could speak—maybe, Ambassador Lyman, you might want to speak to that as well. Who really is calling the shots in Sudan? Are there other people in the administration who present a more benign face to us, the Americans and to the Europeans and to the Africans and everyone, that then can cobble together deals while the master genocidaire who ought to be at The Hague for crimes against humanity and the like, continues to pull the strings.

Again, as I said, when I met with him in 2005 along with Greg we talked humanitarianism, access, Darfur camps, the ending of the hostilities and supporting the Janjaweed.

And what did he talk about just the entire time? Lift the sanctions. Lift the sanctions. I met with Secretary Kerry when he was still Chairman John Kerry when he was still on the Senate side. He was asking for sanctions relief there. So another question would be the origin of this. Was it a good positive, natural evolution of now is the time to make a deal to try to help the humanitarian crisis or was this something that was sought after for a long time that gives us a semblance of maybe a better situation there but maybe it doesn't?

They're rearming and building up their capabilities like Iran now, becoming far more menacing and ominous if they get that capability, buying more battle tanks and fighter jets.

And you, Mr. Dettoni, in your testimony you make reference to the Enough Project and their new report entitled "Border Control from Hell," how the new migration partnership legitimizes Sudan's militia state.

Now, for seemingly a very selfish reasons, the EU is selling this capability to mitigate the flow of, and here it is—without objection, we'll put the—parts of it, certainly the executive summary in—but they're able to mitigate the flow of refugees when we are providing them a capability that could be used for far more nefarious purposes. So if you could speak to that.

And then you make the statement, Mr. Dettoni, and the others might want to speak to this, on the issue of humanitarian access to the two areas, South Kordofan and Nuba Mountains and the Blue Nile State, "I do not believe any humanitarian access has crossed the battle lines from Khartoum into the two areas."

Is that still accurate as of today, in all of your opinions? That would be an important part of this. And, again, why January 13th? Was that the natural time when this came to fruition for the administration to make this decision?

To hand an incoming administration a well thought-out policy that came to its natural fruition on January 13th to promulgate this or was it—should it have been done 6 months ago or not at all and wait for the new administration? I'm baffled by the timing of it.

As you're going out the door you say, here, take this. It may be very well crafted but I would appreciate your insights on that and these other questions again, like who's in charge for real in Khartoum. Mr. Brooks-Rubin.

Mr. BROOKS-RUBIN. Thank you, Chairman Smith.

There's a lot there. I guess let me just try to answer a couple and if I missed I will keep coming back.

In terms of the purchases that we've seen, reports and information about what's happening on the ground continue to come in and we are happy to provide more information on those purchases of interest.

I think the bigger point is and one of the debates around the sanctions lifting is is this really going to matter—does this really change the economic situation on the ground.

And I think one thing that's important and reflective of purchases like these are it opens up the ability for there to be one-time purchases like this. Maybe long-term investment remains questionable because of the overall business environment in Sudan.

But now the banking channels are open. Now without fear of transactions being rejected or blocked by a bank along the way.

So you create an enabling environment that then allows the regime to then decide what it's going to do and, again, from our assessments so far, although there have been the cessation of hostilities that's been discussed, the long-term planning that envisions the sanctions being removed altogether is looking ahead to the ability to make these kinds of weapons purchases and really entrench itself further.

What we are doing by this policy is essentially enabling the regime to just simply entrench itself further without creating any mechanism to have these discussions about a broader democratic process and peace process in the country, which in some way leads me to the Iran question. And you're absolutely right that human rights have been sort of consistently left off the table in all of these situations.

I think what's notable in the Iran example is that we still do maintain a pretty significant level of sanctions. Not all, and certainly has enabled quite a lot of activity by the Iranian regime but we still maintain at some level some robust sanctions in place.

With Sudan, we are talking about still taking these limited steps but yet giving away the rest of the existing sanctions program without replacing it with anything, which seems in inapposite and really, again, as you said, Mr. Chairman, giving away the concept of human rights.

Your reference to Ambassador Natsios is a useful one. In preparing for the hearing, I went back and looked at a press conference that he and Deputy Secretary Negroponte and former OFAC Director and Acting Under Secretary Adam Szubin had way back in 2007 when I was at Treasury. When they announced Plan B, which was the rollout of Darfur sanctions, which was really supposed to put pressure on the regime to stop what was happening in Darfur, to stop the genocide, the sanctions that were announced at those times weren't strong.

We were really just identifying companies that were already sanctioned, but we were promised, and Ambassador Natsios' remarks in that press conference really say that we are going to use pressure and we are going to use robust enforcement to really get at these critical issues of human rights and that pressure was the only way to deal with the regime in Sudan and we never saw that happen.

Human rights was never truly tried to pressure in any meaningful way and that's what we think needs to happen now and you need to have these independently verifiable benchmarks around peace and human rights and religious freedom in order to get there.

In terms of the question about sort of where did this come from and where did it originate, obviously, a lot of what was happening within the administration isn't entirely clear but it does seem—certainly seemed to us that this was—at least the decisions at the end about what sanctions relief to put on the table seemed hastily created and, as you said, handing the next administration, here, we are leaving you something that you need to make sure you deal with and to continue the process going.

Obviously, something was needed in order to keep the Sudanese engaged. But it certainly did not ever appear to be, as you were indicating, may have been preferable, a well—a long, explained and thought out process.

This was something that was really only announced at the very end and there wasn't the level of deliberation and at least engagement with the NGO community that we had at the very end and the Executive order says there has to be consultation with the NGOs, moving forward.

But what that process was, why we got there wasn't really ever clearly established. So I think I will stop with those for now and happy to come back and address the others.

Mr. SMITH. Who's in charge? Did you want to touch on that?

Mr. BROOKS-RUBIN. Who's in charge? I think that's a question maybe others may be better placed to answer than me specifically. I think it is a real question that I think we all struggle to really understand and I think as we've looked at the violent kleptocratic network that the regime and its insiders have established, clearly, you have to deal with President Bashir.

But there are a lot of other key actors, key advisors and really these entities like the NISS and key corporations that really also play and important role and I think we haven't really talked about the impact of the Gulf and the dynamic between the way the Government of Sudan the shifting alliances between Iran and the Gulf and the role that the countries in the Gulf play both in terms of investments that they have, or if you want to call them investments, essentially giveaways by the Government of Sudan in exchange for cooperation.

So I think the role of the Gulf is also critical to explore here in terms of the broader picture of who's in charge.

Ambassador LYMAN. Thank you, Mr. Chairman.

Let me try to deal with some of these questions as well. Who calls the shots? Well, I think it's always been a mistake for people to underestimate President Bashir.

He has solidified his control. He's managed to move people around when they get too powerful. Not long ago he dismissed two very powerful people, Vice President Taha and Nafi Ali Nafi, and who knows, they may come back 6 months from now. They were both very powerful people.

There are two military organizations. There's the regular military and there's the NISS, which controls the militias, the so-called Janjaweed. Now it's called the RDF or whatever it's called. So you have power centers there, all of which the President uses to, frankly, maintain his own position, protect his own interests, et cetera. He's appointed a Prime Minister, Prime Minister Bakri.

Bakri is someone very close to the President. I think he feels that Bakri is someone who will also protect his interests.

So you have an autocratic system but with someone who plays powerful interests against each other. Now, it also is true, going to another question, that there are people with different opinions about where the country ought to go.

There are a number of people who understand that the system that they've been operating for a long time, where you keep the outlying areas at bay through fighting, through co-optation, through exploitation, whatever, keeps the power at the center, is draining the country and will keep draining the country. They've got people like former Minister Ghazi and others who have spoken out on this and written about how to democratize the country, et cetera.

There are also people who want a better relationship with the United States and understand. There are other people who feel very, very differently—that all our talk about human rights and peace, et cetera, is a danger to the security of the regime.

And as long as they consider human rights and accommodation a danger to the security of the regime, they're going to fight against it. And the difficulty for us outsiders is how do you engage in that situation and you try engage, encouraging the people who are thinking differently and trying to counter the arguments of those on the other side and it's going to be slow and it's going to be a very difficult process and we have to keep working with it.

Now, the origin of the—actually it's a product of about 2½ years of debate inside the administration—first, whether we should have such a dialogue at all, whether the Sudanese are open to it. And you have to remember that my successor, Don Booth, couldn't get a visa to Sudan for over a year.

So the question was how do you relate? It was a long tough debate and then toward the end what are the elements of the debate. Got to the end of the administration. They put it out there and I realize it puts suddenly something on the next administration.

I think the 6 months is because these are very limited conditions, very limited benchmarks, and if you had them out there for a year it could last but not move you any farther, at least that's my interpretation. You have to ask the people.

Now, I'd like to talk a little bit more about humanitarian access because some of us for many years have been fighting this issue of humanitarian access and others have, et cetera.

But it has been a political football by both sides. Okay. Sometimes the opposition says that is our number-one concern and sometimes they say well, it has to be linked to the political dialogue.

There are people in the government who don't want humanitarian access because they do believe that, you know, that without it it weakens the opposition. They're also afraid of weapons being coming in and all of that.

But we are very close to an agreement on—"we" I say under Thabo Mbeki—very close to an agreement on humanitarian access and the opposition said, okay, we are all for it except it has to come—at least some of it has to come from Ethiopia. It can't just all come from Sudan.

Now, you can argue as to whether you think that was a worthwhile condition to hold it all up. The governments didn't agree with that and both of them are playing games because it's related to whether they're really willing to move beyond that to a political dialogue.

And the people who suffer are the people in the two areas, and I'm personally unsympathetic with both sides on this particular issue.

But it does go to the complexity of this—of the negotiations. Humanitarian access really has to be linked to an understanding in the two areas that it's not a one-time thing.

It's got to be part of a process where you have a cessation of hostilities and have a political process. If it's a one-time thing it'll break up in 6 months and it won't have accomplished more than that immediate——

Mr. DETTONI. Piggy-backing on some of your comments, I agree, that the cease-fire and the humanitarian assistance have got to be linked for it to last and I think that's the justification.

We've seen some hope because the fighting has really slowed or ceased and for me, we do need to try to give peace a chance. Unfortunately, we have to incentivize Khartoum.

I also think Khartoum has played America very well. I mean, very good poker players. I wouldn't go to a casino if they were dealing and I mean that as respect for their intellect and their capability and as far as Bashir and the people he's got in power.

I think that they assume that we forget. I think that they could overwhelm us with problems and complexities, but at the end of the day I do agree, who's still in power? Mr. Bashir.

Hassan al-Turabi, who was the intellectual—the power, the brains, whatever you call it, behind the National Islamic Front when they—when they took over Bashir and he took over power in 1989. But he's dead. Mr. Bashir's still in power.

And I've heard anecdotally from other people who have been close to Mr. Bashir that he knows what he's doing. He knows the people around him. He knows very well how to play them off of each other and how to stay in power.

I also think that we do need to look at their actions, not what they say. They'll say what we want to hear. I think they'll say to diplomats what we want to hear and smart diplomats, wise diplomats like Ambassador Lyman know that.

For instance, religious freedom, Mr. Wolf said it, you said it—it's the canary in the coal mine, particularly in regions like Khartoum and the issues that are going on there.

All we have to do is look at the past several months. You know, the Czech pastor who was arrested—complicated reasons why. He snuck in, took footage, they caught him when he was in Khartoum—not the smartest thing to do, and I don't—but still.

But then they arrested two Sudanese pastors who evidently were at a religious freedom conference in Addis. The intelligence network for Khartoum were there videotaping it, like they're probably in the crowd here videotaping this, and so they locked them up when they went back to Khartoum.

So for me, the nature of that what's called a government, a regime, is that they fundamentally, I don't think, believe in religious freedom. Hassan al-Turabi changed his tune about 10 years ago, started writing about religious freedom because we were down there talking to him.

Other people were talking to him. He said, you thought I could curry favour with the West. But I think you have to look back to the 1990s with what they did to justify their violent and militant attacks against America and our allies and the type of people that are willing to do that, and they're still in power, what are they really about. And I think we need to know that.

Now, we also need to give peace a chance. We can't just forget it and walk away, and we led the peace process with President Bush for the South and for Sudan and we have a moral obligation but it's also in our security interest to do so.

You had asked about the humanitarian assistance, if anything has gone in through the battle lines and, to my knowledge, no— that crossed the front lines, no.

Ambassador Lyman, I think you already touched on some of the rationale behind it. I've heard that the opposition looked at what happened in Darfur and they said no way, we are not allowing that to happen again.

I don't know all the details about what happened in Darfur but I heard that security really controlled what was going in and what was going out.

And I know that, like, in a lot of other countries, not just in Sudan, but Sudan looks at refugees as a security issue and you don't know which aid workers to the Red Crescent or whoever else like that is working for their intelligence service or for some security apparatus there.

If you walk as a Catholic bishop or a Catholic priest with a truckload of grain or something like that, whatever, that's pure humanitarian goods and gets to go in, the chances of you getting that through, in my opinion, all of it through would be slim.

On the refugee situation, specifically to Eritrea that I wrote about, I had a European official who works on refugee issues tell me—I said, oh, you know, I said, oh, you have—you have a lot of Eritrean refugees coming to Europe—that must—you must be excited about that, what have you.

And he's, like, no, no, no, we are not—we don't want them. They can't speak any—they're not—they're very unskilled, very uneducated. They're traumatized from what happened to them when they had to perform—serve in the military.

And the report that you all did at Enough, it catalogues the state that the Europeans don't want the Eritreans coming because they're a threat to their society to have them there because they could be lost, they're uncontrolled and that sort of thing.

Lastly, I think that the—I have great respect—I've never served as Special Envoy. The pressures that are there are—and the kind of work that you have to do, very difficult.

I think that Special Envoy Booth—I didn't understand it but he sort of in a very—cerebral, smart but I think he lost control when he was at the USIP giving comments before he left and he singled out the SPLM-North particular for—and blamed them for the humanitarian assistance agreement falling apart.

I don't think envoys should do that very often and I think what he said was, these people—and he also was referring to other—all of the leaders are serving themselves more than their people.

But then as Ambassador Lyman said in his remarks, the SPLM-North itself is having some issues right now. One of the top figures wants self-determination—ill-defined, whereas some of the others say no, we belong as a unified—John Garang's vision of a new Sudan—democratic participation.

And so I felt like that they were pushing so hard for whatever reason—maybe for Mr. Obama's legacy. I don't understand why. But I think that, you know, whoever takes over as envoy, whoever inherits his portfolio within the Trump administration is going to have to walk some of that back.

The other thing—I've said it before but it's—we have a lot of dedicated career professionals in the State Department and all over. But, you know, right now our Africa policy and our Sudan and South Sudan policy is rudderless and it won't have a rudder until Mr. Trump gets his people in key positions.

And so I don't think if I were Khartoum or if I were the opposition members I wouldn't—if I got an email from—or a conversation from somebody in the State Department right now, I wouldn't pay any attention to it.

I'd say, you know, put a Trump person in there, then I will deal with you. It'd be the same if it was, you know, a Democratic administration. You got to have your own people in to do the work and have some guidance from the top in order to have the credibility and to get some things done.

So I think we are in a real holding pattern and that's another reason why I suggest 180-days long or a year because it's going to take a few more months until we get some key people in at the White House and in the bureaucracy to handle these issues.

Mr. ABUBAKR. I would like to get back to you about all these points in writing in detail.

Mr. SMITH. Sure.

[The information referred to follows:]

WRITTEN RESPONSE RECEIVED FROM MR. MOHAMED ABUBAKR TO QUESTION ASKED DURING THE HEARING BY THE HONORABLE CHRISTOPHER H. SMITH

As always, whoever is footing the bill. Nowadays that happens to be Saudi Arabia. GoS greatest survival tool/skill throughout the past 27 years has been shapeshifting . By pulling strings of all ideologues in the region, by sounding exactly like them in their line of thinking when it's needed, Al-Bashir managed to extort solidarity funds to keep his regime afloat. There's absolutely no doubt that Saudi Arabia's has the greatest influence on the decision to ease sanctions on Sudan. Similarly, Saudi Arabia has everything to do with what will follow in Sudan internally and its behaviors regionally. Exactly like Iran did before Al-Bashir sold them out. The new government that will be announced is to formalize the new direction and ideology adopted by the regime after they (once more) switched their allegiance.

Truth is, GoS' Alpha and Omega is money. Self-enrichment is what this government is all about, and it would change its behaviors and ideology in any way that would grant more access to more funds. While that's terrible party to engage with, I think it's also one that can be made to comply, using a very simple quid-pro-quo formula that directly ties human rights, religious freedom, and civil liberties enhancement to access to funds would without a doubt work, and work effectively. The assumption that human rights and religious freedoms will always be rejected by the government of Sudan is simply wrong. It will be dismissed if it's on the table along with other items that they can pretend to deliver on (like peace process, for example).

Mr. ABUBAKR. But I want to build on one point that was made about the question of who's in charge.

I definitely agree it's al-Bashir who's in charge and I think where this is coming from, what is calling the shot at the end of the day I believe it's not ideology or for power.

I think it's money, at the end of the day, and I think the only way to get that kind of change in human rights and religious freedom, as Ambassador Lyman said, if there are elements in there that will always push and push aside human rights as something that is part of something on the table and I think the way to go about it is to make human rights profitable, to make it the thing on the table, the main thing, and religious freedom and human rights the thing to negotiate about, not something additional on the table that they can cast aside. And that's all I want to say about that.

Mr. SMITH. Thank you.

We are almost finished because we do have to be out of here by 5:00. But I just wanted to ask maybe a lightning round here. Do we need a Sudan Special Envoy again?

I'm thinking of introducing a bill. It shouldn't take a bill. The President could do it with a snap of his fingers. But is that needed? Is it a recommendation you would make?

Secondly, Juba and South Sudan—and Greg and I were in Juba last August meeting with Salva Kiir, pressing these issues of humanitarian access to end the sexual violence, now, sadly, a famine.

That has taken the eyes off of Khartoum and put them squarely to the South. Has Khartoum then exploited that lack of scrutiny that they are not getting to the degree they used to?

Are the church leaders and that would include Muslim, Christian, the imams, all the church leaders, are they being used effectively in any kind of interfaith effort or is that a nonstarter?

And finally, UNAMID, we met with UNMISS when we were in South Sudan. The Security Council has made some very significant changes to their operating procedures, especially after the debacle in the Terrain compound and when they did not act and I did have the privilege of speaking to the Security Council.

I was invited, as I said earlier, by Nikki Haley to be at the Blair House, be one of four members presenting.

And I pointed out, they were obviously the ones that are in charge of this ultimately, they made some very significant systemic reforms. Hopefully, they pan out well, going forward.

But UNAMID, your thoughts on that. Is their mandate sufficient? Are they doing what they should do? And then anything you'd want to add please do and then we'll conclude.

Ambassador LYMAN. I could start quickly on that. Thank you.

You know, I think the administration is reviewing how many Special Envoys they ought to have and for what purposes. I think in this case there should be a Special Envoy, empowered, as Mr. Dettoni had said, because the kind of negotiations that need to be done on both Sudan and South Sudan require high-level attention.

Has to be someone who speaks for the President. People know he speaks or she speaks for the President and can engage on hard negotiations in both north and south.

You know, there wasn't this much attention to Sudan lately as—and thank you for this hearing because South Sudan is such an overwhelming problem. But I think it's coming back as we look at this EO and the issues that are being raised and the kinds of the decisions.

But I do think it's important when you talk about Sudan it goes to the question Mr. Garrett raised, they are players in the South Sudan situation. They've pulled back on some of their support for the opposition. That was part of the understanding in this track. But there's much more to be done on South Sudan. IGAD is di-vided.

They are major players in IGAD. I would like to see them step up much more constructively.

On UNMISS, I think they have improved in management but they are limited. Right now, they are overwhelmed with their protection of the people who are writing those POCs—they're called protection of civilian areas.

They don't really intercede between the government and the opposition. The fighting is going on. They don't have quite the capacity, let alone the mandate.

So they are not—they're relevant and can be more relevant for protection. They're not relevant, quite frankly, to stopping the fighting.

Mr. SMITH. Thank you all for your expertise. If nobody else wants to comment, let me just say——

Mr. BROOKS-RUBIN. Maybe just 2 seconds on the envoy question. I apologize.

I think we generally would agree with that. I think the bigger issue is what Mr. Dettoni said is in order to have an envoy who's going to really make an impact you need a policy and until there are policymakers clearly in place, an envoy runs the risk of not being able to advance a clear policy and not being taken seriously, as Mr. Dettoni said.

So, I think our perspective is if there is a clear policy and a strong policy and then someone who can clearly and strongly carry it out with the clear backing of the administration that is clear to Khartoum has the backing of the administration as, again, Mr. Dettoni made clear, then that's important and I think the last point I wanted to make by jumping in is this is where there is, clearly, a role for Congress and, clearly, a role for this committee to make clear what are the priorities and what needs to be done now in this while there is this uncertainty.

This is really when Congress needs to act and take the mantle by establishing what are the policies that really matter and what are the mechanisms and measures we need in order to achieve them.

So I think that's ultimately where we can move on.

Mr. SMITH. Does that mean new legislation or just——

Mr. BROOKS-RUBIN. It could, yes. I mean, it should—it should—it should—it should mean legislation. There is a proposal that I think would have a lot of these measures in them and outline the diplomatic track that's needed to get at the human rights and peace track that we talked about.

So yes, it's legislation, it's also clearly indicating to the administration these are what the priorities are. But we——

Mr. SMITH. You did say in your testimony it should be delinked from the five tracks.

Mr. BROOKS-RUBIN. Yes.

Mr. SMITH. Why wouldn't it be incorporated?

Mr. BROOKS-RUBIN. Well, I think from our perspective, the five tracks have their own trajectory. They have their own limited set of issues they're dealing with. What we are talking about are much bigger issues that need much different pressures.

And so in some ways let's not muddy the waters on either side. Let's keep two sets going so——

Mr. DETTONI. Sudan, South Sudan—the whole issue has traditionally had very good bipartisan support. In a town right now that's, as you know better than we, it's hard to work with the other party, whichever party you're in right now.

This is a winner as far as bipartisan approach, and I know that you're willing to work on the issues with everybody.

But the President and others, this could be a winner and a good way to develop some relationships because, you know, at the end of the day, working with the other side of the aisle is always about relationships, not always about party politics.

I want to underscore what I wrote in the testimony what Ambassador Lyman said, if a tree falls in North Carolina I'm not blaming Khartoum.

This was their policy for years and years and years to destabilize South Sudan. The rebel movements—they were very good at it in the North, South, call it that war. They have a network. They have the capability to run everybody and they can run circles in some ways around and destabilizing South Sudan.

So if you're able to get that classified review I would really ask to know the history of that to the extent that you have the time to listen and to know what's halted, in their opinion, and what's continued.

And this needs to be on the table because the two countries, they were one country for a long time. They're linked. Their futures are linked. If they're not getting along then there's going to be destabilizing and massive humanitarian issues.

So that's one thing I would not let go of.

Mr. SMITH. It's an excellent point. Yesterday, Greg and I did get a classified briefing. We want to include others and now that we have even more questions to ask we'll do another one.

But it's a great idea because we always want to not do something unwittingly to damage what is being done if it's been well thought out. So I can't talk about the briefing, obviously, but we did have one yesterday.

But your point is very well taken about getting Royce, Engel, Karen Bass and I and others all to do it. Thank you for that.

I deeply appreciate—we appreciate it at the subcommittee. Your information, we will get it over to State but, more importantly, to some of the people at the White House.

Obviously, we benefit from your expertise and wisdom—Congress and the executive branch. So thank you so very, very much. The hearing is adjourned.

[Whereupon, at 4:59 p.m., the subcommittee was adjourned.]

A P P E N D I X

<small>Material Submitted for the Record</small>

70

SUBCOMMITTEE HEARING NOTICE
COMMITTEE ON FOREIGN AFFAIRS
U.S. HOUSE OF REPRESENTATIVES
WASHINGTON, DC 20515-6128

Subcommittee on Africa, Global Health, Global Human Rights, and International
Organizations
Christopher H. Smith (R-NJ), Chairman

April 26, 2017

TO: **MEMBERS OF THE COMMITTEE ON FOREIGN AFFAIRS**

You are respectfully requested to attend an OPEN hearing of the Committee on Foreign
Affairs, to be held by the Subcommittee on Africa, Global Health, Global Human Rights, and

Sudan Relief Fund

Mr. Mohamed Abubakr
President
The African Middle Eastern Leadership Project

The Honorable Princeton N. Lyman
Senior Advisor to the President
United States Institute of Peace

By Direction of the Chairman

COMMITTEE ON FOREIGN AFFAIRS

MINUTES OF SUBCOMMITTEE ON _Africa, Global Health, Global Human Rights, and International Organizations_ HEARING

Day __Wednesday__ Date_____ _April 26, 2017_ _____Room _2200 Rayburn HOB_

Starting Time ___ _2:32 p.m._ ___ Ending Time ___ _5:00 p.m._ ___

Recesses | _1_ | (_3:01_ to _3:43_) (____to ____) (____to ____) (____to ____) (____to ____) (____to ____)

Presiding Member(s)
Rep. Chris Smith

Check all of the following that apply:

Open Session ☑
Executive (closed) Session ☐
Televised ☑

Electronically Recorded (taped) ☑
Stenographic Record ☑

TITLE OF HEARING:

The Questionable Case for Easing Sudan Sanctions

SUBCOMMITTEE MEMBERS PRESENT:

Rep. Tom Garrett, Rep. Dan Donovan, Rep. Tom Suozzi, Rep. Karen Bass

NON-SUBCOMMITTEE MEMBERS PRESENT: _(Mark with an * if they are not members of full committee.)_

HEARING WITNESSES: Same as meeting notice attached? Yes ☑ No ☐
(If "no", please list below and include title, agency, department, or organization.)

STATEMENTS FOR THE RECORD: _(List any statements submitted for the record.)_

Border Control from Hell report from the Enough Project, submitted by Rep. Chris Smith

TIME SCHEDULED TO RECONVENE _____
or
TIME ADJOURNED ___ _5:00 p.m._ ___

Subcommittee Staff Associate

MATERIAL SUBMITTED FOR THE RECORD BY THE HONORABLE CHRISTOPHER H. SMITH, A REPRESENTATIVE IN CONGRESS FROM THE STATE OF NEW JERSEY, AND CHAIRMAN, SUBSUBCOMMITTEE ON AFRICA, GLOBAL HEALTH, GLOBAL HUMAN RIGHTS, AND INTERNATIONAL ORGANIZATIONS

The project to end genocide and crimes against humanity

Cover photo: RSF troops in their armed vehicles
East Jebel Marra, January 2, 2015.
Photo: Sudan Armed Forces

Border Control from Hell
How the EU's migration partnership legitimizes Sudan's "militia state"

By Suliman Baldo
April 2017

Executive summary

Large-scale migration to Europe has precipitated a paradigm shift in relations between the European Union (EU) and the government of Sudan, and closer ties between both entities. This new partnership has resulted in the EU disbursing millions of euros to the Sudanese government for technical equipment and training efforts geared toward stopping the flow to Europe of migrants from Sudan and those from Eritrea, Ethiopia, Somalia, and other countries in sub-Saharan Africa who come through Sudan.

The EU's action plan will involve building the capacities of Sudan's security and law enforcement agencies, including a paramilitary group known as the Rapid Support Forces (RSF), which has been branded as Sudan's primary "border force." The EU will assist the RSF and other relevant agencies with the construction of two camps with detention facilities for migrants. The EU will also equip these Sudanese border forces with cameras, scanners, and electronic servers for registering refugees.[1]

There are legitimate concerns with these plans. Much of the EU-funded training and equipment is dual-use. The equipment that enables identification and registration of migrants will also reinforce the surveillance capabilities of a Sudanese government that has violently suppressed Sudanese citizens for the past 28 years.[2]

Sudan's strategy for stopping migrant flows on behalf of Europe involves a ruthless crackdown by the RSF on migrants within Sudan. Dogged by persistent armed uprisings led by opponents protesting chronic inequalities in the distribution of national wealth and political power in its periphery regions, the Sudanese government has always relied on a plethora of militia groups to counter insurgencies. The RSF is one of these militia groups. It evolved from the disparate Janjaweed militias that carried out the genocidal counterinsurgency policy of the Sudanese regime in Darfur that began in 2003. However, in its functions and evolution, the RSF differs significantly from other militia groups employed by the government.

---

1 The Enough Project • enoughproject.org
   Border Control from Hell:
   How the EU's migration partnership legitimizes Sudan's "militia state"

The RSF first evolved from a strike force deployed against insurgents in Darfur into a national counterinsurgency force under the operational command of Sudan's National Intelligence and Security Services (NISS) that was tasked with fighting the Sudan People's Liberation Movement/Army-North (SPLM/A-N) in South Kordofan and Blue Nile states. Then, in September 2013, the RSF was deployed against peaceful demonstrators who were protesting the Sudanese government's removal of subsidies on basic commodities. More than 170 people were killed in September 2013,[3] in incidents that unmasked the Sudanese regime's dependence on the militia to quell political dissent and marked a new evolution in the role of the RSF.

Starting in 2015 and 2016, and convinced of the RSF's effectiveness as a counterinsurgency force, the regime designated the RSF as Sudan's primary force tasked with patrolling Sudanese borders to interdict migrants' movement. The Sudanese government made this designation within the framework of its partnership with the EU for the control of migration. As such, the RSF is positioned to receive EU funds for reducing the flows of migrants from Sudan to Europe. The Sudanese government enacted a law in January 2017 that integrated the RSF into the Sudan Armed Forces (SAF, national army). The 2017 law (conflictingly) made the RSF autonomous, integrated into the army, and under the command of President Omar al-Bashir (see below).

The EU and the EU member states that are most engaged with Sudan in the actual programmatic partnership on migration flows should scrutinize the record and conduct of the RSF as the partnership unfolds. By "building the capacity" of Sudan's newly minted border force with funding and training, the EU would not only be strengthening the hand of the RSF but also could find itself underwriting a complex system of a "militia state"[4] that Sudan has evolved into since the current regime came to power in 1989. In so doing, the EU contradicts and undermines the overriding objectives of its own founding treaty. EU members cannot advance peace, security, and human rights and they cannot stem irregular migration from Sudan and the Horn of Africa by directly funding a government that deploys a militia group that stokes violent conflict, commits atrocities, and creates massive displacement of populations within Sudan.

The remainder of this paper synthesizes public information about the RSF's activities and argues how EU support for this group could ultimately worsen irregular migration to Europe, escalate violent conflict within Sudan and the Horn of Africa, and embolden a regime and militia force that acts with impunity and now faces even fewer checks on its criminal behavior. This paper aims to highlight the latest developments from Sudan and examine the record of earlier engagements of the RSF, lest one or all of Sudan's EU partners claim, at a later date, that they were unaware of the perverse incentives at play.

Introduction

The relations between the European Union as a whole and individual countries outside the EU, including Sudan, are governed by the provisions of the EU's external action, set forth in the 1992 Treaty on European Union. These provisions enshrine the principles of "democracy, the rule of law, the universality and indivisibility of human rights and fundamental freedoms, respect for human dignity, the principles of equality and solidarity, and respect for the principles of the United Nations Charter and international law."[5]

In 2011, the EU adopted a strategic framework to guide its engagement with the Horn of Africa, stating that the EU would "work with the countries of the region and with international organizations (especially the United Nations and African Union) to resolve current conflicts, particularly in Somalia and Sudan, and avoid future potential conflicts between or within countries."[6] Adopted formally in

2   The Enough Project • enoughproject.org
   Border Control from Hell:
   How the EU's migration partnership legitimizes Sudan's "militia state"
The complete version of this document can be accessed here: https://go.usa.gov/xN8va